TRANSPORTATION ISSUES, POLICIES AND R&D

U.S. FREIGHT TRANSPORTATION

ELEMENTS, ROLE AND RECOMMENDATIONS FOR IMPROVEMENT

TRANSPORTATION ISSUES, POLICIES AND R&D

Additional books in this series can be found on Nova's website under the Series tab.

Additional e-books in this series can be found on Nova's website under the e-book tab.

TRANSPORTATION ISSUES, POLICIES AND R&D

U.S. FREIGHT TRANSPORTATION

ELEMENTS, ROLE AND RECOMMENDATIONS FOR IMPROVEMENT

ALAINA HUTSON
EDITOR

New York

For permission to use material from this book please contact us:
Telephone 631-231-7269; Fax 631-231-8175
Web Site: http://www.novapublishers.com

Library of Congress Cataloging-in-Publication Data

ISBN: 978-1-63321-235-0

Published by Nova Science Publishers, Inc. † New York

CONTENTS

PREFACE

Transportation is important. It is about people and how they live their lives, how they get to work, how they get their children to school, how they buy food, clothes, and other necessities, and how families visit one another around the country. It is also about business. Transportation is critical to how the supply chain functions, how raw materials get to factories, how goods get to market, how food gets from farmers to kitchen tables, and how energy products move from areas of production to areas of consumption. An efficient national transportation network allows business to lower transportation costs, which lowers production costs and enhances productivity and profits. It allows American business to be competitive in the global marketplace and for the Nation's economy to prosper and grow. One need only look at the Interstate Highway System to see how that investment in the transportation network has benefited the nation and encouraged tremendous economic growth over the past two generations. This book discusses findings and recommendations made by the Special Panel on 21st century freight transportation, as well as federal freight policies.

Chapter 1 – The Panel on 21st Century Freight Transportation conducted hearings, held roundtable discussions, and traveled to key freight corridors across the United States to gain insight into the current state of freight transportation and how improving freight transportation can strengthen the economy. The Panel identified many challenges and impediments to the efficient and safe movement of goods into, out of, and through the United States.

The Panel found that the current state of highway infrastructure does not adequately serve the needs of those moving goods across the Nation. Not every community is located adjacent to a railroad, airport, waterway, or port, but a consumer good is almost invariably transported along the Nation's four million miles of highways and roads for at least part of its journey. However, the Highway Trust Fund, from which federal investment in highway infrastructure is disbursed, will soon be insolvent. This fact is especially problematic when one considers that maintenance of the Nation's existing highway facilities alone would cost hundreds of billions of dollars, and that one of every four bridges in the United States is structurally deficient or functionally obsolete. Furthermore, a recent study found that congestion cost the United States economy $121 billion in 2011.

Chapter 2 – This is the Statement of Derek J. Leathers, President and CEO, Werner Enterprises, Inc. Hearing on "Overview of the United States' Freight Transportation System."

Chapter 3 – The U.S. freight system is a complex network including four principal modes of transportation:

- The National Truck Network comprises 209,000 miles of highways that can accommodate large trucks, including the 47,000-mile Interstate Highway System.
- Railroads, largely in private ownership, carry freight on 140,000 miles of track.
- Barge and ship lines utilize 12,000 miles of shallow-draft inland waterways and about 3,500 inland and coastal port terminal facilities.
- Air carriers provide cargo service to more than 5,000 public use airports, including more than 100 airports that handle all-cargo aircraft.

About two-fifths of freight within the United States, measured in ton-miles, moves by truck, and another two-fifths moves by rail (*Figure 1*). About 11% moves by multiple modes. Measured in ton-miles, air transportation is a minor mode because it is expensive to ship goods this way. Goods moving by air tend to be of high value compared to their weight. About three-quarters of U.S. imports and exports, measured by weight, arrive or depart by ship. Most of the rest goes by truck (10%), rail (8%), or pipeline (5%). International air shipments account for less than 1% of U.S. foreign trade by weight, but 37% by value.

In: U.S. Freight Transportation
Editor: Alaina Hutson
ISBN: 978-1-63321-235-0

Chapter 1

IMPROVING THE NATION'S FREIGHT TRANSPORTATION SYSTEM: FINDINGS AND RECOMMENDATIONS OF THE SPECIAL PANEL ON 21ST CENTURY FREIGHT TRANSPORTATION*

Panel on 21st Century Freight Transportation

EXECUTIVE SUMMARY

The Panel on 21st Century Freight Transportation conducted hearings, held roundtable discussions, and traveled to key freight corridors across the United States to gain insight into the current state of freight transportation and how improving freight transportation can strengthen the economy. The Panel identified many challenges and impediments to the efficient and safe movement of goods into, out of, and through the United States.

The Panel found that the current state of highway infrastructure does not adequately serve the needs of those moving goods across the Nation. Not every community is located adjacent to a railroad, airport, waterway, or port, but a consumer good is almost invariably transported along the Nation's four million miles of highways and roads for at least part of its journey. However,

---

* This is an edited, reformatted and augmented version of a report released by the House Committee on Transportation and Infrastructure, dated October 2013.

the Highway Trust Fund, from which federal investment in highway infrastructure is disbursed, will soon be insolvent. This fact is especially problematic when one considers that maintenance of the Nation's existing highway facilities alone would cost hundreds of billions of dollars, and that one of every four bridges in the United States is structurally deficient or functionally obsolete. Furthermore, a recent study found that congestion cost the United States economy $121 billion in 2011.

While most consumer goods are transported on a truck for at least part of the journey, freight rail provides efficient long-haul and short-haul service and integrates closely with the trucking industry. There are approximately 565 freight railroads in the country employing nearly 180,000 workers. These are privately owned companies that operate more than 200,000 miles of track throughout the Nation. Because the freight railroads are private entities, they own the infrastructure over which they operate, meaning they also invest heavily in those networks. In 2011, the freight railroads invested over $23 billion in capital expenditures to improve and expand their networks.

Before goods can be transported on trucks or railroads, the goods must be produced, and many of these goods are produced overseas. Over 75 percent of all United States international freight moves by water. Unlike the Highway Trust Fund, the federal fund dedicated for harbor maintenance has a positive balance. Unfortunately, a lack of appropriated funding has resulted in deferred maintenance of federal channels that serve coastal ports. Currently, the constructed depths and widths of entrance channels at 59 major ports are available only 35 percent of the time. Given the current expansion of the Panama Canal and the larger ships that will service American ports as a result, maintaining authorized channel depths and widths is critical to the stability of the Nation's import and export market.

United States waterways carried an equivalent of over 100 million truckloads of goods last year. It is estimated that without the barges and towboats operating on the inland waterways, the Nation would need 6.3 million railroad cars or 25 million trucks to haul the difference. However, much of the critical infrastructure for waterborne transportation is in dire need of repair. More than one-half of the locks and dams in the United States are over 50 years old.

Air cargo is the fastest way to ship goods over long distances, and air freight is high-value cargo. Less than three percent of total freight by weight ships by air, but this represents over $6.4 trillion worth of goods per year, which is nearly 35 percent of all freight value.

All aspects of the supply chain rely on the warehousing, distribution center, and logistics industry. Logistics is the planning, execution, and control of a complex organization involving many different moving pieces and interests, all within a system designed to achieve specific objectives. By optimizing the movement of freight across all modes of transportation, this industry helps ensure the health of the United States economy and the future of the Nation's global competitiveness.

The Panel found that ten percent of the Nation's freight movement, by tonnage, travels through pipelines. Pipelines, by their very nature, specialize in the transmission of energy commodities. In that regard, pipelines carry nearly two-thirds of the Nation's energy supply. Today, there are over 2,600,000 miles of pipelines in the United States—enough to circle the globe about 100 times.

As a result of these findings, the Panel makes the following key recommendations. To safely and efficiently meet the needs of freight movements in the 21st Century, Congress should:

- Direct the Secretary of Transportation, in coordination with the Secretary of the Army and the Commandant of the United States Coast Guard, to establish a comprehensive national freight transportation policy and designate a national, multimodal freight network;
- Ensure robust public investment in all modes of transportation on which freight movement relies, and incentivize additional private investment in freight transportation facilities, to maintain and improve the condition and performance of the freight transportation network;
- Promote and expedite the development and delivery of projects and activities that improve and facilitate the efficient movement of goods;
- Authorize dedicated, sustainable funding for multimodal freight Projects of National and Regional Significance through a grant process and establish clear benchmarks for project selection. Projects eligible for such funding would have a regional or national impact on the overall performance of the multimodal freight network identified by the Secretary of Transportation;
- Direct the Secretary of Transportation, in coordination with the Secretary of the Treasury and the Secretary of the Army, to identify and recommend sustainable sources of revenue across all modes of transportation that would provide the necessary investment in the

Nation's multimodal freight network and align contributions with use of, and expected benefit of increased investment in, such network; and
- Review, working through the Committee on Transportation and Infrastructure and the Committee on Ways and Means, the Secretary's freight funding and revenue recommendations and develop specific funding and revenue options for freight transportation projects prior to Congress' consideration of the surface transportation reauthorization bill in 2014.

This report includes a detailed discussion of the Nation's freight network and makes recommendations that will improve the safety, efficiency, and performance of the nation's freight transportation system.

INTRODUCTION

Transportation is important. It is about people and how they live their lives, how they get to work, how they get their children to school, how they buy food, clothes, and other necessities, and how families visit one another around the country. It is also about business. Transportation is critical to how the supply chain functions, how raw materials get to factories, how goods get to market, how food gets from farmers to kitchen tables, and how energy products move from areas of production to areas of consumption. An efficient national transportation network allows business to lower transportation costs, which lowers production costs and enhances productivity and profits. It allows American business to be competitive in the global marketplace and for the Nation's economy to prosper and grow. One need only look at the Interstate Highway System to see how that investment in the transportation network has benefited the Nation and encouraged tremendous economic growth over the past two generations.

The federal government has historically played a strong role in transportation. In fact, one of the events that precipitated the Constitutional Convention was a longstanding dispute between Virginia and Maryland regarding navigation rights on the Potomac River impacted by transportation improvements proposed by President George Washington.

President Washington determined that the new Nation must have the transportation infrastructure in place to facilitate effective trade and communications. However, Washington's efforts to extend navigation required a formal treaty between Maryland and Virginia, as well as elaborate approvals from other states in the Continental Congress. To settle that dispute he called for a convention to be held in Annapolis in 1786 to address problems with the Articles of Confederation and how the young Nation would move forward on this issue of navigation rights. That summit failed, but it demonstrated to the participants the need to improve the Articles of Confederation.

It was in this context that the Constitutional Convention was called and the Constitution itself drafted. The framers of the Constitution recognized that the Articles of Confederation were not meeting the transportation and commerce needs of a young Nation. The Constitution addressed this issue primarily in the Commerce Clause, which gives the Congress the power to regulate interstate commerce and create, in the words of the Preamble, "a more perfect Union".[1] Furthermore, Article I, Section 8, clause 7 of the Constitution requires the Congress to establish post offices and post roads.[2] The post roads of the1780s and 1790s became the highway and byway system that the Nation enjoys today.

Over the years, the Nation has continued to invest in critical transportation infrastructure, from the Transcontinental Railroad to the Panama Canal to the Interstate Highway System. The reason for this continued investment in the transportation network is to ensure that the Nation is connected, supporting the needs of the Nation's economy and the American people.

As President Dwight D. Eisenhower observed, without the unifying force of commerce and transportation, the United States would be a mere alliance of many separate parts. President Washington recognized this truth in the earliest days of the union, and the Congress must renew its commitment to providing a robust physical platform upon which the American people and American businesses can prosper.

In 2011, the United States transportation system moved 17.6 billion tons of goods, valued at more than $16.8 trillion.[3] The Federal Highway Administration estimates that in the next 30 years, there will be 60 percent more freight that must be moved across the Nation.[4] To keep up with such demand, it is critical that Congress seek ways to increase the efficiency, safety, and overall condition and performance of the Nation's freight network.

Given the multi-modal nature of freight movement, it is important to examine the system as a whole. Goods frequently move back and forth between ocean vessels, highways, railroads, air carriers, inland waterways, ports, and pipelines. Bottlenecks arising at any point on the system can seriously impede freight mobility and drive up the cost of the goods impacted. For this reason, improving the efficient and safe flow of freight across all modes of transportation is critical to the health of the United States economy and the future of the Nation's global competitiveness.

To illustrate this point, in testimony before the Panel on June 26, 2013, United Parcel Service Chief Operating Officer David Abney outlined the movement of a package from New York to Germany. For the manufacturer to receive supplies from California, assemble the good, and send it to its final destination involves 10 distinct freight movements involving three modes of transportation – rail, truck, and air.

In testimony before the Senate Committee on Commerce, Science, and Transportation on June 18, 2009, Rick Gabrielson, Senior Director of International Transportation of the Target Corporation, provided another telling example that demonstrates the intermodal nature of goods movement.[5] A simple tee-shirt manufactured overseas moves by truck and ocean vessel before entering the United States at a United States port. It is processed at a nearby sorting facility, where it is combined with similar items arriving from other foreign points of origin. These items are then loaded onto trucks or trains and delivered to a distribution facility, at which point the shirt is combined with other items designated for the same destination. These items are then transported via truck or train, depending on the distance between the distribution facility and the destination. If a customer wants a product shipped directly to their residence or business, Target may utilize cargo aircraft to transport the goods, in addition to trucks, trains, and vessels. Due to the complexity of the supply chain, even the smallest delay at any point can cause massive ripples throughout the system, resulting in significant economic loss.

HIGHWAYS AND TRUCKING

The Nation's highway system is an essential part of the freight network. Not every community is located adjacent to a railroad, airport, waterway, or port, but a consumer good is almost invariably transported along the Nation's four million miles of highways and roads for at least part of its journey.

History of the Highway System and the Highway Trust Fund

Federal assistance for highway construction began in the early 20th Century when Congress provided $500,000 for highway construction in the Postal Service Appropriations Act of 1912.[6] In 1944, Congress authorized significant expanded federal assistance for construction of a "National System of Interstate Highways".[7] Without a dedicated source of revenue, however, construction of the Interstate System stalled.

The landmark Federal-Aid Highway Act of 1956 and Highway Revenue Act of 1956 authorized significant funding for a 41,000-mile National System of Interstate and Defense Highways and established the Highway Trust Fund (HTF) as the mechanism for financing the accelerated highway investment.[8] To finance the increased authorizations, the Revenue Act increased federal excise taxes paid by highway users and provided that these revenues should be credited to the Highway Trust Fund. This dedicated funding mechanism provided financial certainty for the highway program, including the Interstate Program. The 13-year authorization of the 1956 Act gave the states and highway construction industry the continuity needed to develop and build highway projects.

At its inception, the excise rates for highway use of motor fuels, also known as the gas tax, were 3 cents per gallon. Over the years, however, the tax rate and structure have been revised numerous times, most recently in 1993. Current rates set the gas tax at 18.4 cents per gallon of gasoline and 24.4 cents per gallon of diesel.[9]

Until major revisions in 1982, all receipts from motor fuel taxes were deposited into the HTF. The Surface Transportation Assistance Act of 1982 increased the tax rates from 4 cents per gallon to 9 cents per gallon, established separate Highway and Mass Transit accounts within the HTF, and deposited 1 cent out of the 9 cents per gallon into the Mass Transit Account.[10] Currently, of the 18.4 cents per gallon federal excise tax on gasoline, 15.44 cents is deposited into the Highway Account, 2.86 cents is deposited into the Mass Transit Account, and 0.1 cent is deposited into the Leaking Underground

Storage Tank Trust Fund. Of the 24.4 cents per gallon federal excise tax on diesel, 21.44 cents is deposited into the Highway Account, 2.86 cents is deposited into the Mass Transit Account, and 0.1 cent is deposited into the Leaking Underground Storage Tank Trust Fund. The latest Federal Highway Administration data show that HTF net receipts (excluding General Fund transfers) totaled $40.1 billion in fiscal year 2012, with $35.1 billion deposited into the Highway Account, and $5.0 billion into the Mass Transit Account.[11]

Without an increase in receipts, the cash balance in the Highway Account of the HTF has fallen dramatically.[12] Congress addressed this need for more investment by significantly increasing authorization levels for high-way programs in the Transportation Equity Act for the 21st Century (TEA-21), the Safe, Accountable, Flexible, Efficient Transportation Equity Act: A Legacy for Users (SAFETEA-LU), and most recently in the Moving Ahead for Progress in the 21st Century Act (MAP-21).[13] When SAFETEA-LU expired at the end of fiscal year 2009, the Federal Highway Administration (FHWA) reported that the balance in the Highway Account was $8.8 billion. However, steps were not taken to increase receipts into the HTF, and the cash balance in the HTF has fallen dramatically. To maintain the solvency of the HTF, between fiscal year 2008 and fiscal year 2014, Congress transferred approximately $54 billion from the General Fund to the HTF.

Unfortunately, current Congressional Budget Office (CBO) projections show that the cash balance in the Highway Account will be depleted sometime in fiscal year 2015. According to CBO, in fiscal year 2015, the Highway Trust Fund revenue will be less than $39 billion, while expenditures will total more than $53 billion.[14] These figures do not capture the full extent of the Trust Fund shortfall because FHWA will also have to outlay funds for projects for which funding was obligated in previous fiscal years. This cash shortfall is projected to continue in subsequent years if left unaddressed, with CBO estimating that the HTF will face a cash deficit of $132 billion over fiscal year 2012 to fiscal year 2023.[15]

The Interstate System was established as a cost-to-complete system. As a general rule, each route was required to meet certain design specifications. Every state was provided federal funding to cover 90 percent of the cost of constructing its route segments.[16] The states were responsible for the remaining 10 percent of the construction cost, as well as for all costs associated with the operation and maintenance of the system.[17] Through the creation of the Highway Trust Fund and the financing of construction of the Interstate System, the Federal-Aid Highway Act and Highway Revenue Act gave birth to the modern era of federal involvement in highway infrastructure, known as the Federal-aid Highway Program.[18]

The Federal-aid Highway Program is a federally assisted, state-managed and -operated program in which the states are responsible for the planning, design, and construction of highway projects, as well as operating and maintaining major roads. The federal government provides financial resources and technical assistance to state and local governments for constructing, preserving, and improving the National Highway System (including the Interstate System) and other urban and rural roads that are eligible for federal aid.

With the enactment of Intermodal Surface Transportation Efficiency Act (ISTEA), the Interstate System was declared complete with only a few short segments remaining to be constructed.[19] The final ISTEA funds for these segments were apportioned to the states in fiscal year 1995.[20]

Governments at all levels invested $182 billion in 2008 for highways and bridges in the form of capital outlay, maintenance, highway and traffic services, administration, highway safety enforcement, and debt service.[21] In fiscal year 2012, the federal capital investment in highways totaled $39.9 billion.[22]

However, this level of investment continues to fall far short of the needs of our surface transportation system. According to the United States Department of Transportation (DOT), to maintain the Nation's highway system at a state of good repair and improve it to meet future demand, all levels of government need to increase outlays specifically for capital investment from $91 billion to $170 billion annually over a 20-year period. This estimate does not include operations and maintenance costs.[23]

Bridges on the Nation's highway system are also in serious need of increased investment. According to DOT, one of every four bridges in the United States is structurally deficient or functionally obsolete. Of the 607,380 bridges in the United States, 151,497 are deficient, including 66,749 structurally deficient bridges and 84,748 functionally obsolete bridges. The backlog of cost-beneficial bridge investment is $121.2 billion.[24] To eliminate the backlog of deficient bridges over the next 20 years, DOT estimates that annual investment in bridge repair and replacement must increase from $12.8 billion in 2008 to $20.5 billion annually.[25]

Economic Impact of the Highway System

Approximately 50 percent of all freight tonnage moved in the United States travels less than 100 miles between origin and destination.[26] At this distance, trucks carry almost 85 percent of all of the freight that is moved.[27] More than 250 million vehicles traverse the highway system each year, and commercial trucking requires a reliable highway system on which to operate.[28] However, each day approximately 12,000 miles of the highway system slow below posted speed limits and an additional 7,000 miles experience stop-and-go conditions.[29] Such congestion negatively impacts the efficiency of the highway system as a reliable mode of transportation.

Moreover, America's reliance on the highway system is growing faster than the system itself. National public highway mileage increased at an average rate of 0.2 percent between 1997 and 2010, while total vehicle miles travelled grew to an average annual rate of 1.3 percent during the same period.[30] Congestion has increased as a result of this disparity.

The Texas Transportation Institute's (TTI) *Urban Mobility Report* found that congestion in 498 of the Nation's cities cost the economy $121 billion in 2011, or nearly $750 for every commuter in the country.[31] This figure is up from an inflation-adjusted $24 billion in 1982.[32] Of the $121 billion, $27 billion of the delay cost is the effect of congestion on truck operations.[33] Furthermore, congestion is becoming a problem that transcends "rush hour," with about 40 percent of the Nation's delay occurring in the mid-day and overnight hours, creating an increasingly serious problem for businesses that rely on efficient production and delivery.[34] TTI estimates that in 2011, the amount of fuel wasted in congestion nearly reached 2.9 billion gallons—enough to fill the New Orleans Superdome four times.[35]

In its recent Traffic Scorecard, INRIX made a startling discovery. It found that in 2013, 61 of the Nation's 100 most congested cities have experienced increased traffic congestion over the prior year.[36] This is a dramatic shift from 2012, where only 6 cities experienced increased congestion and 94 saw decreases in congestion levels.[37]

The congestion challenges in Southern California provide a sobering example of the tangible harm that congestion inflicts on the Nation's economy. More than 43 percent of the Nation's containerized imports enter the country through Southern California.[38] The import and export traffic of the Southern California ports benefit the residents of every region of the United States. Goods imported and exported through Southern California make their way to and from each state, supporting billions of dollars of local economic activity and millions of jobs.[39]

When congestion, bottlenecks, and other inefficiencies hinder the Southern California region's ability to import goods through its maritime ports and international border crossings or its ability to move these goods through the region, costs rise and transit times increase. These costs are often passed on to consumers. Consequently, the level at which the freight network functions in Southern California tangibly impacts the lives of consumers all across the Nation.

Furthermore, according to a recent study, more than 16 million jobs in the United States depend on imports.[40] This study does not even take into consideration the millions of additional domestic manufacturing jobs that rely on an efficient freight transportation network to export American-made goods.

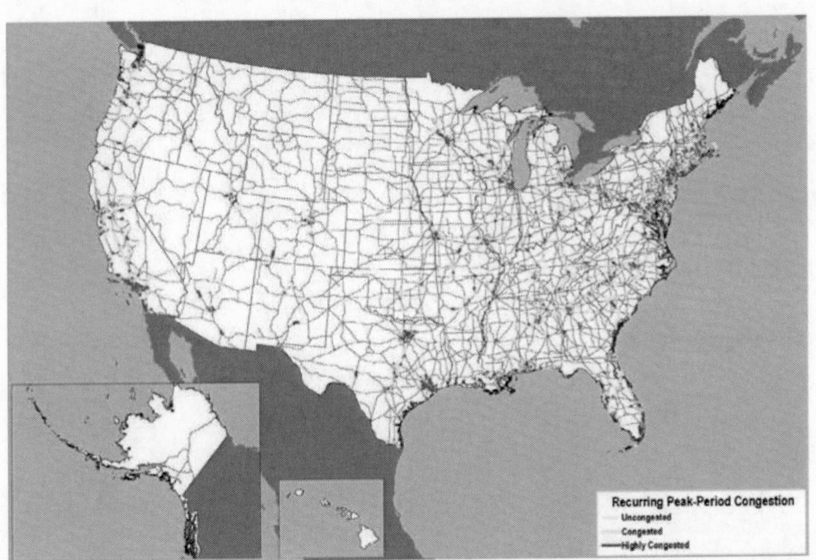

Note: Highly congested segments are stop-and-go conditions with volume/service flow ratios greater than 0.95. Congested segments have reduced traffic speeds with volume/service flow ratios between 0.75 and 0.95

Source: U. S Department of Transportation, Federal Highway Administration, Office of Highway Policy Information, Highway Performance Monitoring System, and Office of Freight Management and Operations, Freight Analysis Framework, version 2.2, 2007.

Peak-Period Congestion on the National Highway System: 2002.

Comparing the costs of transporting soybeans to China from the United States and to China from Brazil illustrates the critical role that the Nation's freight system plays in the global competitiveness of American industry. Currently, it costs $85.19 to transport one metric ton of soybeans from Davenport, Iowa, to Shanghai, China.[41] It costs $141.73 to transport the same amount of soybeans approximately the same distance to Shanghai from North Mato Grosso, Brazil. The United States currently enjoys a competitive advantage because the Nation's freight system is more efficient and cost effective than Brazil's system. However, Brazil is planning to invest $26 billion to modernize its freight facilities. These advances will dramatically decrease the cost of moving Brazilian soybeans to market. Without an efficient, highly functioning freight network, American businesses will lose their competitive advantage in the global marketplace.

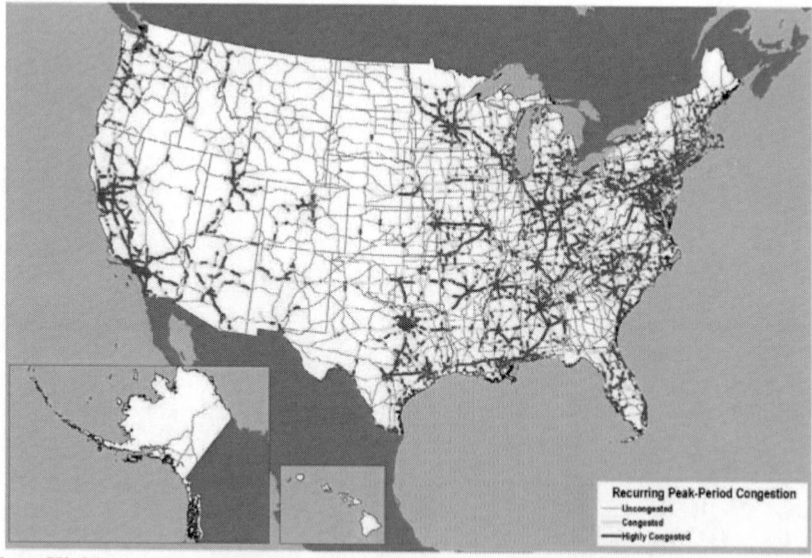

Note: Highly congested segments are stop-and-go conditions with volume/service flow ratios greater than 095. Congested segments have reduced traffic speeds with volume/service flow ratios between 0.75 and 0.95.

Source: U. S. Department of Transportation, Federal Highway Administration, Office of Highway Policy Information, Highway Performance Monitoring System, and Office of Freight Management and Operations, Freight Analysis Framework, version 2.2, 2007.

Pak-Period Congestion on the National Highway System: 2035.

In 2011, the Nation's transportation system moved 17.6 billion tons of goods, valued at over $16.8 trillion.[42] Given the connected nature of the Nation's supply chain, the issues that impact the freight systems in urban areas have a direct impact on the economic competitiveness of the entire Nation.

In addition to congestion, a bridge collapse or closure brings significant and sudden economic impacts to the affected region. In the wake of the I-35W bridge collapse in Minnesota in 2007, the road user costs due to the unavailability of the river crossing averaged $400,000 per day. The Minnesota Department of Transportation further found that Minnesota's economy lost $17 million in economic output in 2007 and $43 million in 2008 as a direct result of the bridge collapse.[43] Similarly, on May 23, 2013, the I-5 Bridge over the Skagit River in Mount Vernon, Washington, collapsed after it was struck by a truck. The Washington Department of Transportation estimates that the total direct cost of the 26-day closure of the I-5 Skagit River Bridge was $8.3 million.

FREIGHT RAIL

Freight railroads move large quantities of goods throughout the country. The railroads played a seminal role in the development of the United States and in the industrial revolution, and this mode continues in its vital importance to the movement of goods into and across the Nation. Railroads are an integral part of North America's infrastructure network and, in turn, the Nation's economic competitiveness.

History of the Freight Rail System

Freight railroads have played a tremendously important role in the annals of United States history. Railroads have moved goods across the Nation before trucks or planes existed and to areas unreachable by ship. The ability to move people and goods via rail directly aided the development of the Western states, and it contributed to the development of new products and markets that improved the Nation's economic vitality and competitiveness.

While the use of carts with metal wheels running on railed tracks dates back to the mid-1700s, the advent of the steam-powered locomotive revolutionized the cheap and efficient movement of goods. John Fitch, an American already famous for designing the first steam-powered boat, designed and built the first working steam-powered locomotive in 1794.[44] The early-1800s saw numerous technological innovations to rail infrastructure as companies sought ways to move goods to areas not served by the Nation's canal system.

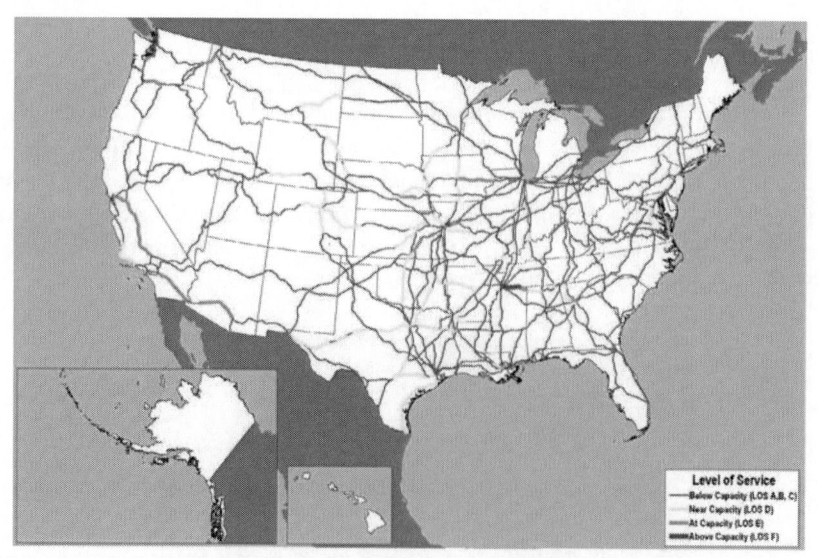

Note: Level of Service (LOS) A through F approximates the condition described in Transportation Research Board, *Highway Capacity Manual 2000* period.

Source: Association of American Railroad. *National Rail Infrastructure Capacity and Investment Study*, prepared by Cambridge Systematics, Inc. (Washington, DC. September 2007), figure 4.4, page 4-10.

Current Train Volumes Compared to Current Capacity.

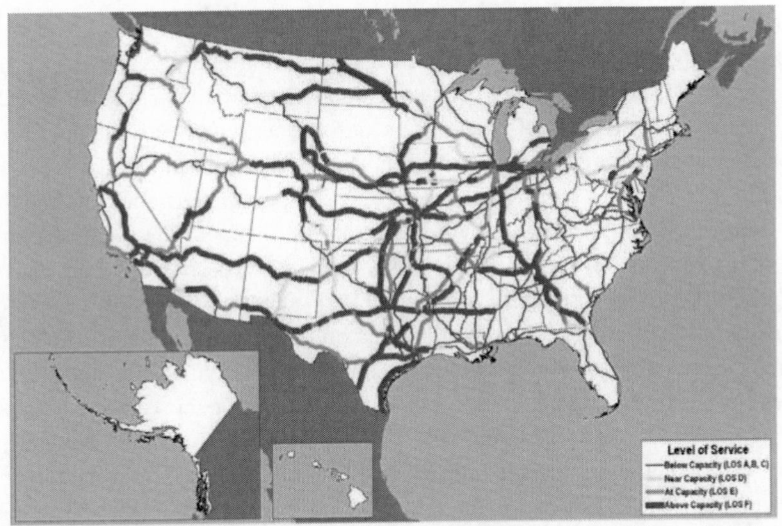

Note: Level of Service (LOS) A through F approximates the conditions described in Transportation Research board, *Highway Capacity Manual 2000*.

Source: Association of American Railroads, *National Rail Infrastructure Capacity and Investment Study*, prepared by Cambridge Systematics, Inc. (Washington, DC. September 2007), figure 5.4, page 5-5.

Train Volumes in 2035 Compared to Current Capacity.

President Abraham Lincoln recognized the benefits of a nationwide rail system and worked with Congress to pass the Pacific Railroad Act of 1862 (12 Stat. 489).[45] This law authorized construction of the Transcontinental Railroad, which was completed in 1869, less than seven years after the law's enactment. In the 150 years since the passage of the Act, the railroad system has expanded to serve all areas of the Nation.

Today, freight railroads are divided into three groups, called classes, based upon their annual revenues. While Class I railroads generally provide long-haul freight services, the Class II and III railroads often provide the first and last mile of rail freight movements.

Economic Impact of the Freight Rail System

America's freight railroad network is the envy of the world. There are approximately 565 freight railroads in the country employing nearly 180,000 workers.[46] These are privately owned companies that operate over more than

200,000 miles of track throughout the Nation.[47] Freight railroads are divided into three groups, called classes, based upon their annual revenues. A Class I railroad is defined as having an annual carrier operating revenue of $250 million or more; a Class II railroad is defined as having an annual carrier operating revenue between $20 million and $250 million; and a Class III railroad is defined as having an annual carrier operating revenue of less than $20 million.[48] In accordance with federal regulations, the annual carrier operating revenue is measured in 1991 dollars.[49] There are seven Class I freight railroads that operate in the United States: BNSF Railway; CSX Transportation; Canadian National; Canadian Pacific; Kansas City Southern; Norfolk Southern; and Union Pacific.[50] The majority of railroads, however, are Class II and III railroads, known generally as regional or short-line railroads.

While Class I railroads generally provide long-haul services, the Class II and III railroads often provide the first and last mile of rail freight movements. The products moved by rail include everything from automobiles, agricultural goods, and consumer products to chemicals, lumber, and energy resources. In all, freight rail carries 43 percent of intercity freight, which is more than any other mode, and for every one rail job, 4.5 other jobs are supported elsewhere in the economy.[51] Furthermore, the Department of Commerce estimates that for every $1 invested in the Nation's rail system, the industry returns $3 to the economy.[52]

Unlike other modes, the freight railroads own the infrastructure over which they operate, meaning they also invest heavily in those networks. In 2011, the freight railroads invested over $23 billion in capital expenditures to improve and expand their networks.[53] This investment is due in large part to the movement toward de-regulation of the freight railroads beginning in the 1970s through the Staggers Rail Act of 1980 (P.L. 96-448), and culminating in the Interstate Commerce Commission Termination Act of 1995 (P.L. 104-88).[54] Deregulation allowed the freight railroads to price competitively and respond to market forces, which has increased productivity, enhanced safety, lowered average rates, and freed over $500 billion for private investment back into the freight network.[55] Furthermore, particular to the Class II and III railroads, deregulation has grown that industry from 8,000 miles of track in 1980 to over 51,000 miles today.[56] Class II and III railroads are now the feeder and distribution lines for the network, reaching into small town, rural America to preserve those areas' connection to the national network.

As noted above, the United States freight railroad industry employs nearly 180,000 workers. More than 160,000 are employed by the seven Class I freight railroads and another 20,000 are employed by the 558 short line and regional freight railroads.[57]

The United States rail industry is heavily unionized. Approximately 85 percent of Class I employees and around 60 percent of non-Class I employees belong to a union and thus are subject to collective bargaining agreements.[58] Collective bargaining agreements between railroads and their employees are governed by the Railway Labor Act, which was first passed in 1926.[59] Collective bargaining for most other industries is governed by the National Labor Relations Act.[60]

Most Class I railroads and a number of non-Class I railroads bargain on a "national handling" basis. National handling covers more than 90 percent of the Nation's unionized rail employees.[61] Under national handling, a group of railroads acting as a unit negotiates with a union or group of unions for an agreement that applies to all those who participate in the bargaining. The members of each union, however, must ratify their contracts on an individual basis once a tentative agreement is in place. There are currently 13 major unions that represent rail workers.[62]

SHIPPING AND PORTS

Moving people and goods over water is arguably the oldest form of transportation in human history. For millennia, civilizations have depended upon ships to move goods to support nations and economies. Today, the shipping industry is one of the most sophisticated freight networks in the world, transporting the vast majority of goods in international trade and employing millions of people across the globe.

The United States has essentially four coastlines that are responsible for importing and exporting commodities from around the world: the East Coast, the West Coast, the Gulf Coast, and the Great Lakes. Commercial navigation through the Arctic Ocean along the north coast of Alaska looms as a potential fifth coast. From our coastal ports, goods move across the country, primarily by rail and truck. Getting products to market in an efficient and safe manner is critical to keeping the economy moving and requires extensive intermodal coordination.

History of the Shipping and Port System

Shipping has had a prominent role in American history from the Nation's inception. Were it not for the importance of shipping and trade, European explorers would not have discovered North America in search of a navigable route to Asia. Additionally, the maritime industry's ability to quickly and reliably transport raw materials and agricultural products from the colonies to Europe encouraged the development of North America in the 1600s. Ocean shipping provided a direct connection between the colonies and the rest of the world, facilitating trade and encouraging exploration and development of the continent's vast natural resources.

Over the years, in a continual effort to stay competitive, the shipping industry has evolved in recognition of changing commodities and emerging markets, global or regional armed conflict, challenges with shipping long distances, integrated global trading partners, changing ocean shipping economic conditions, including the emergence of extremely large vessels, and demands for new products from international sources.

While there have been many technological innovations to ships and ports that improved the efficiency, range, and capacity of the maritime industry, the invention of the intermodal container by Malcolm McLean in 1955 revolutionized the industry by allowing for standardization of cargo.[63] Intermodal containers are reusable steel boxes with standard sizes and connection points that allow for multiple uses on ocean-going cargo ships, trucks, and freight trains. Due to the superior efficiency of this shipping approach, global standardization resulted and containers became the unit of volume used to define the capacity of ships or ports. Today, the twenty-foot equivalent unit (TEU), referencing the size of the standard intermodal container, is now the standard industry metric. The freight industry generally, including ships, trucks, and trains, has been standardized to accommodate the safe and efficient transfer of these containers between transportation modes.

Prior to the use of containers to transport manufactured goods, maritime cargo was primarily loaded by hand in bulk pallets. Containerization allowed the shipping industry to gain efficiency in three main areas and, consequently, expand exponentially. First, the use of containers allowed for the quick movement of goods between ship and shore and between truck and train without having to break down and repackage the goods. Second, containers could be unloaded and loaded on various modes of transportation much more quickly than before through the use of larger, more efficient gantry cranes. Third, the use of containers greatly increased the freight volume capacity of the entire freight system. For example, ocean-going vessels could stack containers on a ship's deck and transport more goods than was previously possible by loading cargo only in a ship's holds.

In addition to containerization, other types of ships have evolved over the years to meet special cargo and transport needs. Today, the world's oceans are plied by a wide assortment of ship types including dry bulk carriers for coal, iron ore, and lumber; specialized ships for hauling agricultural products; fuel tankers for oil and natural gas; roll-on/roll-off car and vehicle carriers; and a variety of specialty ships designed to transport specific commodities, such as wind turbines.

The shipping industry is continually seeking ways to maximize its efficiency in transport, including fuel use, while taking into consideration the specific harbors that a ship services. Ships carrying cargo to or from Pacific Rim countries must continually balance ship design and size with the constraints of the Panama Canal and the logistical constraints of transiting the Mediterranean and Red Seas through the Suez Canal. The constant demands for reducing fuel consumption on the open sea and increasing safety in transiting the ingress and egress of straits, approaches, and harbors require a high level of training among licensed mariners and crew. The shift to ship designs that use more automation technologies has helped to improve efficiencies without sacrificing navigation safety.

Economic Impact of the Shipping and Port System

Cargo ships move massive amounts of goods and commodities around the world every year. Over 75 percent of all United States international freight moves by water.[64] The United States is the world's largest importer of containerized goods and the world's second-largest exporter of such cargo.[65] For the Nation to continue importing and exporting such a large volume of goods and commodities, integrated port infrastructure and land-side connections are necessary. In addition, it is vital to invest in the navigation tools and technologies necessary to provide mariners with accurate real-time information to safely and efficiently access and egress the Nation's ports and waterways. Moreover, port security and maintaining security throughout the supply stream require an integrated and transferable way to track and maintain control over goods in transit.

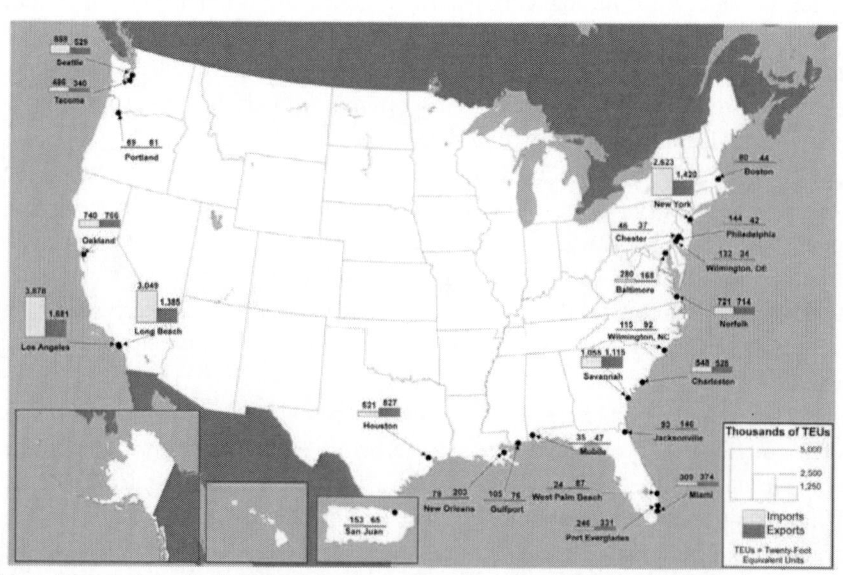

Note: The statistics include both government and non-government shipments by vessel into arid out of U.S. foreign trade zones, the 50 stales. District of Columbia, and Puerto Rico.

Source: U.S. Department of Transportation, Maritime Administration, U.S. Waterborne Container Trade by U.S. Custom Ports, based on data provided by Port Import/Export Reporting Service, available at www.marad.dot.gov/library_landing_page/data_and_statistics/Data_and_Statistics.htm as of August 29, 2011.

Top 25 Water Ports by Containerized Cargo: 2010.

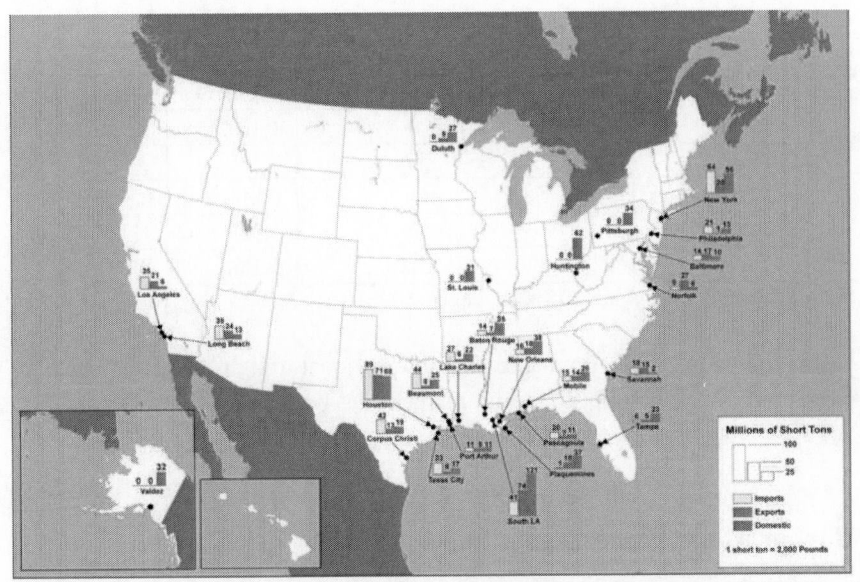

Source: U.S. Army Corps of Engineers, *2010 Waterborne Commerce of the United States, Part 5, National Summaries* (New Orieans, LA: 2010), table 5-2, available at www.ndc.iwr.usace.army.mil/wcsc/wcsc.htm as of June 18, 2012.

Top 25 Ports by Tonnage: 2010.

The majority of the Nation's bulk commodities and containerized goods are shipped through ports. Ports serve as points of entry for imported goods and egress for exports. After entering harbors, ships move to specific marine terminals that are often specialized to handle the type of ship and cargo being transported. These marine terminals often serve as end points of highway and rail freight movements and must be maintained and improved to support efficient and cost-effective trade.

The Marine Transportation System in the United States serves nearly 8,200 separate commercial cargo-handling docks. These docks include public facilities (owned and managed by state, regional, and local port departments and authorities) and private facilities (common-user terminals and dedicated facilities). According to the American Association of Port Authorities, there are 126 public seaport agencies with jurisdiction over 185 ports.[66]

Distribution of the cargo-handling docks and ports by region are as follows:

Location	Foreign Only	Foreign and Domestic	Domestic Only	Total
Atlantic	33	560	1,193	1,786
Pacific	24	571	1,101	1,696
Gulf	17	559	1,560	2,136
Great Lakes	3	246	402	651
Inland	0	0	1,928	1,928
Total	**77**	**1,936**	**6,184**	**8,197**

Source: United States Army Corps of Engineers.[67]

While large ports dominate the international freight dynamic, smaller ports are critical to supporting and maintaining regional and local economies and sustaining the United States coastwise trade under the Jones Act.

Harbor Maintenance Trust Fund

The Water Resources Development Act of 1986 established the Harbor Maintenance Trust Fund (HMTF) for the operation and maintenance (O&M) of harbors.[68] The Harbor Maintenance Tax (HMT), an ad valorem tax, is collected on maritime imports and is assessed at a rate of 0.125 percent of cargo value ($1.25 per $1,000 in cargo value).[69] The tax revenues are deposited into the Harbor Maintenance Trust Fund from which Congress appropriates funds for dredging harbor channels to cover 100 percent of the United States Army Corps of Engineers O&M costs.[70] In addition to the tax on imported goods, domestic cargo shippers—shipments from United States port to United States port—generate about five percent of the HMT revenues while cruise ships passengers generate less than one percent.[71] Cargo and passengers from Alaska, Hawaii, and other United States territories are exempt from the HMT.[72] Ports on inland rivers are also exempt from the HMT and are assessed fuel taxes that support the Inland Waterways Trust Fund.[73]

Currently HMT revenues pay for all the maintenance dredging costs at harbors up to 45 feet deep.[74] For deeper harbors, the incremental maintenance cost is 50 percent from the HMTF and 50 percent from the local sponsor, usually the port authority.[75] In fiscal year 2011, the HMTF collected $1.38 billion but estimated expenditures totaled only $790 million.[76] As a result of collecting more revenue than expenditures year after year, the HMTF balance is more than $7 billion.[77] As noted above, these funds may only be used for their statutorily-designated purposes. However, because the HMTF is not an "off-budget" account within the federal budget, the large balance is used to make it appear that the Nation's budget deficit is less in a given year.[78]

A lack of appropriated funding has resulted in deferred maintenance of federal channels that serve coastal ports. Currently, the constructed depths and widths of entrance channels at 59 major ports are available only 35 percent of the time.

Global Shipping Challenges

Shipping operators select harbors to call based on a number of factors including reliability, speed, cost, safety, security, value-added service, availability of cargo, and contributions to overall profitability and other business objectives.[79] Ocean carriers have a choice of routes around the globe—they can go around Cape Horn in Africa, the Cape of Good Hope in South America, or through the Suez Canal or the Panama Canal. Over the last several years, two new routes are beginning to open up that could change the dynamics of global ship deliveries—the Northeast and the Northwest passages through the Arctic Ocean. In 2013, more than 400 ships applied for permits to transit the Arctic Ocean for commercial transport.[80] Using the northern sea route along the Arctic Coast of Russia reduces the transit between East Asia and Western Europe by 21,000 kilometers and reduces the time of transit by one-third.[81]

The physical dimensions of the Panama Canal have historically limited the size of ships that can transit across the Pacific to the Atlantic, and reverse. The current size of the Panama Canal limits ships to a depth of 39 feet and a width of not more than 13 containers across. This is the defined "Panamax" dimension.

As ships began to increase in width and depth to accommodate an increased number of containers, the Panama Canal Authority embarked on an expansion of the canal to adapt to "post-Panamax" sized vessels. The expansion of the Panama Canal is scheduled to be completed in 2015 and will allow the next generation of mega-containerships to move between China and the United States East Coast and Gulf Coast ports.

Not all harbors in the United States will be able to handle these post-Panamax sized ships. On the West Coast, the harbors currently able to handle these ships include Los Angeles-Long Beach, California; Oakland, California; and Seattle, Washington.

On the East Coast, Norfolk, Virginia and Baltimore, Maryland are able to handle post-Panamax ships and New York/New Jersey and Miami, Florida are scheduled to be enlarged to accommodate these ships over the next several years. On the Gulf Coast, Houston, Texas, is currently dredging to allow for post-Panamax sized ships. Of concern in the global shipping community is the continued support of key shipping hubs and connectivity to and from the rest of the United States. It is critical that the hub ports have adequate connections to distribution points throughout the country. Of equal concern is the ability at these ports to break down the loads from the mega-container ships and transfer container cargo to feeder vessels that can access and support smaller harbors along the East, West, and Gulf Coasts, and in the future, the Great Lakes, via short sea shipping.

Bulk Commodities

The United States has multiple commodities that are desired on the global market, including coal, iron ore, taconite, wheat, soybeans, corn, fertilizers, timber, and finished wood products. These bulk commodities require specific loading and unloading facilities. As the commerce of these commodities has increased and become more competitive on a global scale, shippers have moved toward increased modernization and specialization on the products that they ship.

The shifting dynamics of coal, in particular, exemplify this shift in demand and the response of the global bulk shipping community, particularly the increasing global demand for United States-mined coal in Asia and Europe. In Norfolk, Virginia, specific mixes of West Virginia coal are increasingly shipped to Rotterdam, the Netherlands, or to the Black Sea for distribution to the rest of Europe.

INLAND WATERWAYS

Inland waterways provide an efficient means of transporting large quantities of goods from points inland to deepwater ports and from ports to inland markets. Many agricultural and manufacturing entities rely heavily on the inland waterway system to move their goods to market.

History of the Inland Waterway System

The inland waterway system in the United States is primarily concentrated in the Eastern, Midwestern, and Pacific Northwest areas of the Nation. The Mississippi River and its tributaries, the Hudson River and the Saint Lawrence Seaway, the Great Lakes, the Chesapeake Bay, the Delaware River, and the Columbia River are the largest components of the inland waterway system in the United States. The inland waterways of the Midwestern area of the United States connect the Gulf of Mexico ports of Mobile and Biloxi, Mississippi, and New Orleans, Louisiana, to the Mississippi River, which in turn connects to the Illinois, Ohio, and Tennessee rivers. The Great Lakes System; the steel production areas of Detroit, Michigan, Chicago, Illinois, and Cleveland, Ohio; and the taconite ore of Duluth, Minnesota are accessed through the Saint Lawrence Seaway. The Seaway allows access to the Atlantic Ocean and Europe. Lastly, the West Coast Sacramento and Columbia/Snake River systems allow direct access to the agricultural resources of the Central Valley of California and the wheat, hops, and other grain fields of eastern Oregon, Washington, and Idaho. The inland waterway system is the conduit that feeds the coastal ports and provides for integrated global transfer and trading of bulk commodities.

From the earliest days of the Nation's history, American farmers, businessmen, and entrepreneurs used flatboats to float bulk commodities along the inland waterways of the United States. This mode of transportation provided a low-cost, low-energy means of moving large quantities of goods around the Nation. Today, the method of transporting goods and persons on the Nation's inland waterway system is largely unchanged. Unlike the deepdraft vessels that are common in the international maritime industry, relatively shallow-draft barges pushed by towboats traverse the Nation's inland waterways. These barges are capable of carrying intermodal containers, bulk agricultural goods, building aggregates, fertilizers, or liquid fuel. Modern barges typically range from 35 feet to 200 feet in length, based on the size and load of their cargo. These barges are typically put together in groups of tows that are then pushed through the inland waterway system by tugboats. They transit the system through a system of locks and dams that allow the barges to navigate both up and down our river systems.

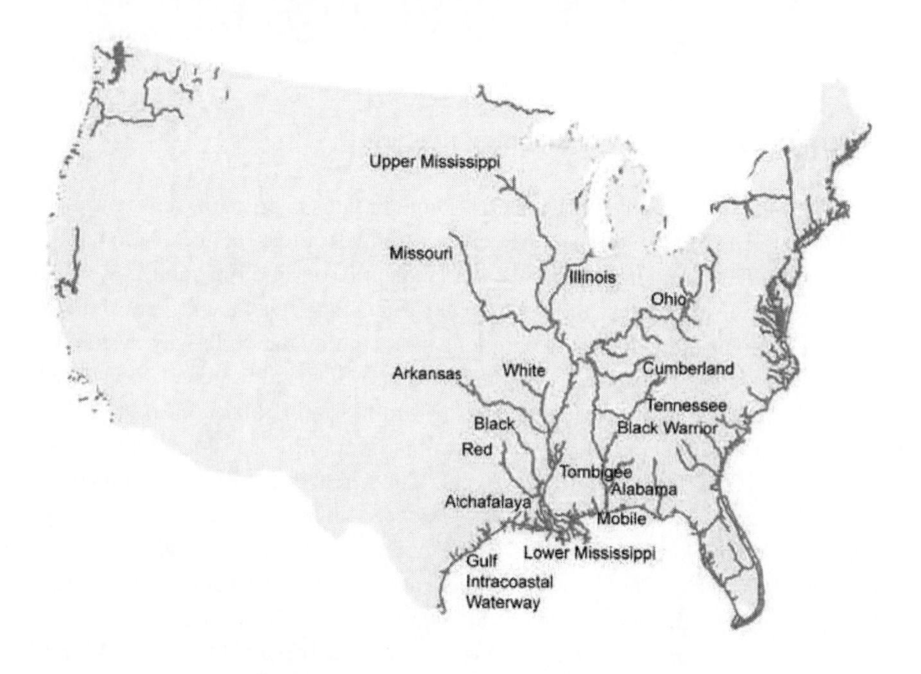

Economic Impact of the Inland Waterway System

The Nation's approximately 12,000 miles of commercially-active, navigable waterways provide an efficient, cost-effective means of transporting goods to domestic and international markets.[82] A tremendous amount of goods are transported on waterways each year, estimated at 2.3 billion tons in 2007.[83] In fact, United States waterways carried an equivalent of over 100 million truckloads of goods last year.[84] However, much of the critical infrastructure for waterborne transportation is in dire need of repair. More than one-half of the locks and dams in the United States are over 50 years old.[85]

Inland waterways transport more than 60 percent of the Nation's grain exports, about 22 percent of domestic petroleum products, and 20 percent of the coal used to generate electricity.[86] In 2010, 566 million tons of waterborne cargo transited the inland waterways valued at more than $180 billion.[87] Local public port districts are economic engines for the communities in which they are located and most are self-sufficient and receive no property or other tax revenue.

It is estimated that without the barges and towboats operating on the inland waterways, the Nation would need 6.3 million railroad cars or 25 million trucks to haul the difference.[88] The domestic maritime industry provides over $100 billion to the Nation's economy in economic output, annually, and provides more than 33,000 jobs aboard its boats and barges alone.[89]

Transporting goods on the inland waterway system also has significant environmental benefits. According to the Tennessee Valley Authority, "Because one barge can transport as much cargo as 15 rail cars or 60 tractor-trailers, waterway transportation benefits the environment. It reduces fuel consumption and emissions, and makes the roads safer by keeping more trucks off of the highways. River transportation has a direct impact on the prices consumers pay for the things they buy. Soft drinks, ice cream, baked goods and pancake syrup, for example, are all sweetened with high-fructose corn syrup made from grain grown in the Midwest."[90]

Inland Waterways Trust Fund

The Inland Waterways Revenue Act of 1978 (26 U.S.C. 9506) and the Water Resources Development Act of 1986 (WRDA 1986; 26 U.S.C. 4042) created the inland waterway financing mechanism. These two Acts established a fuel tax on commercial barges, cost-sharing requirements for inland waterway projects, and the Inland Waterway Trust Fund (IWTF) to hold these revenues and fund these investments. The overall effect of these changes was a greater financial and decision-making responsibility for commercial operators on the inland waterways system.

WRDA 1986 authorized additional increases to the 1978 Act's fuel tax and, pursuant to WRDA 1986, the fuel tax is $0.20 per gallon.[91] The fuel tax has not been indexed for inflation.[92] WRDA 1986 further stipulated that IWTF construction projects would be funded with 50 percent of the funds derived from the IWTF and the other 50 percent from the General Fund.

Under WRDA 1986, expenditures from the IWTF must be authorized by Congress and funded through appropriations acts.[93] WRDA 1986 also established the Inland Waterways User Board, a federal advisory committee, to provide commercial users an opportunity to inform the priorities for United States Army Corps of Engineers decision-making.

From 1986 to today, the balance in the IWTF has varied considerably. Beginning in 1992, balances increased, reaching their highest level in 2002 at $413 million.[94] Beginning in 2005, expenditures began to outpace collections and, concurrently, several projects far exceeded their original cost estimates and balances dropped sharply. Significant concerns have been raised as to the economic viability of the IWTF under the present fuel tax approach. Different solvency proposals have been raised by the Administration and the Inland Waterways User Board.

Case Study: Moving Soybeans from Illinois and Iowa to China

To meet the demands of the soybean market in China, farmers in the Midwest have to coordinate their planting and harvest with the shipment of their crop across multiple modes of transportation. The story begins when the soybeans are harvested in the fields of Iowa and Illinois, usually in September or early October. The soybeans are moved from the field to a barge loading facility on the Mississippi River by trucks or rail. This leg of the journey typically takes one to four days. The soybeans are subsequently loaded onto river barges within one or two days of arriving at the loading facility, and are organized into tows. The journey by barge tow to the New Orleans, Louisiana area typically takes two weeks. The soybeans are then off-loaded to either short-term storage bins or directly onto ocean-going bulk carriers.

The transit to China begins after loading to the bulk carrier. Typically, the coordinated transit of the ship from loading at New Orleans, through transit of the Panama Canal to crossing of the Pacific takes approximately 30 days. After arriving in China, the bulk carrier ship is unloaded and the soybeans are transported via truck or rail to distribution points across China.

The point of this case study is to illustrate the critical nature of coordination and communications in getting a product grown in the Midwest to a market in China. Due to the highly competitive market for soybeans, if the transport system in the United States breaks down or does not produce the desired transportation, the Chinese market will shift from buying Illinois and Iowa soybeans to buying Brazilian soybeans. A loss of two to four weeks in delivery to New Orleans could result in China making an economic decision that will impact the local farmers in the Midwest. An integrated process of moving bulk agricultural commodities is required to keep the economics of the system whole.

AIR CARGO

Air cargo carriers play a vital role in transporting goods both in domestic and international supply chains. Air carriers can move cargo quickly and often move goods of particularly high value. Furthermore, in some areas of the country, air freight is the only reliable means of delivering goods.

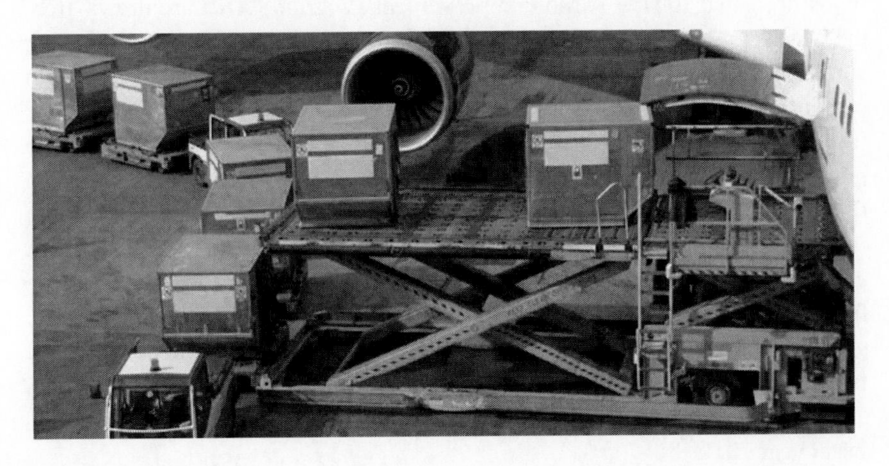

History of the Air Cargo System and the Airport and Airway Trust Fund

Aviation has played a key role in American transportation for more than 100 years. Aviation is often the fastest way to move people and goods around the Nation and the world. Since the earliest days of commercial aviation, shippers have been moving goods via air. In World War II, the military needs of the American forces around the world encouraged many technological advances to the ability of aircraft to effectively move freight long distances. Today, companies like Federal Express and the United Parcel Service maintain extensive fleets of cargo aircraft to move millions of parcels and packages around the world every night.

The Airport and Airway Trust Fund (AATF) was created by the Airport and Airway Development and Revenue Act of 1970 to provide dedicated funding for the Nation's aviation system.[95] Revenues are derived from aviation-related excise taxes on passengers, cargo, and fuel and in turn provide funding for capital improvements to United States airports. The AATF also provides the majority of funding for the Federal Aviation Administration (FAA), estimated at 71.5 percent in fiscal year 2013.[96] The FAA accounts funded include: Operations (funded by the General Fund and AATF); Facilities and Equipment, Research, Engineering, and Development; and Grants-in-Aid for Airports. The AATF also funds the Essential Air Services (EAS) account for the Department of Transportation.

As established by the Airport and Airway Improvement Act of 1982, funds obligated for the Airport Improvement Program (AIP) are drawn from the AATF, which is supported entirely by user fees, fuel taxes, and other similar revenue sources.[97] Some examples of these taxes and fees include: 7.5 percent domestic air passenger ticket tax; $3.90 domestic flight segment tax (up from $3.70); 6.25 percent cargo waybill tax; $17.20 tax on both international arrivals and departures (up from $16.30); 7.5 percent frequent flyer award tax; $8.60 Alaska and Hawaii international air facilities tax (up from $8.20); 19.3 cents per gallon fuel tax for aviation gasoline; 21.8 cents per gallon fuel tax on general aviation jet fuel; 14.1 cents per gallon surcharge on fuel for aircraft used in fractional ownership program (new); and 4.3 cents per gallon fuel tax on commercial airlines.[98] Combined with the revenue generated from interest on the Airport and Airway Trust Fund's cash balance, these taxes and fees generated nearly $11.7 billion in fiscal year 2011 and $12.6 billion in fiscal year 2012.[99]

Economic Impact of the Air Cargo System

Air freight is high value cargo. Less than three percent of total freight by weight ships by air, but this represents over $6.4 trillion worth of goods per year, which is nearly 35 percent of all freight value.[100] Air cargo is transported both in the bellies of passenger aircraft as well as in dedicated all-cargo aircraft on scheduled and nonscheduled service. Currently, there are 33 all-cargo carriers operating 840 cargo aircraft in the United States.[101] In 2012, air cargo carriers flew over 36 billion revenue ton miles (RTMs).[102] Of these 36 billion RTMs, all-car-go carriers comprised almost 80 percent of the total, with passenger carriers flying the remainder.[103]

There are four primary drivers to the air cargo industry—competition, connectivity, cost, and perishability.[104] The competition between carriers keeps the profit margin and the ultimate cost to consumers low. The number of airports across the United States and the world ensure that shippers and consumers can move their goods via air freight. While more expensive than other modes of transportation, the cost of shipping a parcel via air is far from prohibitive. Finally, shippers of perishable and time-sensitive products, such as pharmaceuticals, flowers, or fruits and vegetables, require the air cargo industry, which can reliably deliver goods to market in hours.

Air cargo plays an important role in the quick delivery of goods domestically and internationally. Air cargo provides an efficient way to transfer goods or commodities from one place to another in a short period of time. Due to the volume and price constraints of the air cargo industry, air freight specializes primarily in smaller goods and personal parcels.

WAREHOUSES, DISTRIBUTION CENTERS, AND THE LOGISTICS INDUSTRY

Warehouse, distribution center, and logistics providers play a key role in alleviating inefficiencies and bottlenecks in the Nation's freight system, which can impede mobility and drive up the cost of the impacted goods. By optimizing the movement of freight across all modes of transportation, this industry helps ensure the health of the United States economy and the future of the Nation's global competitiveness.

History of the Logistics Industry

The warehouse, distribution center, and logistics industry adds value to the supply chain by improving the planning, implementation, and control of the flow of goods from point of origin to point of consumption. Today, nearly all of the Nation's top executives have some form of logistics strategy. Every Fortune 100 company, and 80 percent of all Fortune 500 companies, employ at least one third-party logistics (3PL) provider to improve their operations.[105] In 2011, domestic spending in the logistics and transportation industry totaled nearly $1.3 trillion, roughly 8.5 percent of the Nation's gross domestic product.[106] The growth of the logistics industry far outpaces that of the economy at large, further emphasizing the important value that logistics can have in facilitating the efficient movement of goods.[107]

Third-party logistics providers are also known as freight forwarders or transportation intermediaries. Depending on the industry in which a 3PL operates, the 3PL may also be known as a broker (if involved in the trucking industry), a Non Vessel Operating Common Carrier (if involved in the maritime industry), or an indirect air carrier (if involved in the air freight industry). Despite all of these different names, the essential function is the same. At its most basic level, a 3PL is an entity that facilitates the movement of goods.

One of the earliest 3PLs was the Company Limited of London, established in 1836 by Thomas Meadows.[108] Meadows recognized the demand for these intermediary services as the rail transportation and steamship industries expanded. As trade increased between Europe and North America, Company Limited arranged for the transportation of goods from manufacturers to the steamships.[109] The logistics provided by Company Limited, however, soon expanded beyond the mere carriage of goods. Meadows realized the value that additional information could offer, and soon began consulting with his clients on documentation and customs requirements in the country of destination.[110]

Since Company Limited, 3PLs have traditionally operated as non-asset based companies that arranged for the transportation of a shipper's goods with another company that owned and operated a common carrier.[111] Today, many 3PLs also operate their own trucks, aircraft, warehouses, and distribution centers, in addition to offering the traditional logistical advice and analysis that is the hallmark of the industry.[112]

Economic Impact of the Logistics Industry

Logistics is the planning, execution, and control of a complex organization involving many different moving pieces and interests, all within a system designed to achieve specific objectives. According to the Council of Supply Chain Management Professionals, logistics management is the part of supply chain management "that plans, implements, and controls the efficient, effective forward and reverse flow and storage of goods, services and related information between the point of origin and the point of consumption in order to meet customers' requirements."[113]

Put simply, the logistics industry is valuable to the Nation's freight system because logistics improve the efficiency of the supply chain. To name just a few real-world applications, the use of logistics can ascertain the best mode, or combination of modes, to move a particular product to a particular location, give a small carrier access to a large shipper's freight, reduce the number of empty containers a trucking company has to carry, eliminate the need for operating distribution centers in-house, and maximize warehouse layout and productivity.

Another key service of the warehouse, distribution center, and logistics industry are value-added services that improve received products before they are repackaged and shipped to a final destination. Product assembly, inspection, sequencing, re-packaging, and labeling are just some of the many services that the industry provides to add value to the products shipped throughout the world.[114] By carefully collecting and analyzing data about the supply chain, logistics providers can identify areas of lost efficiency and develop strategies to move goods more intelligently.

One of the ways that manufacturers and retailers can maximize the value of 3PLs is through the concept of Just-in-Time Delivery (JIT). The idea behind JIT is that business efficiency will be the greatest when carrying costs are minimized. In other words, by delivering goods at the precise moment when they will be consumed, businesses will not need to pay to store the goods before they are used. JIT relies intrinsically on the logistics industry to efficiently forecast and transport the goods at the moment when they are needed. By avoiding the unnecessary storage of inventory prior to its use, the logistics industry can greatly improve the operating efficiencies of the manufacturing and retail industries.

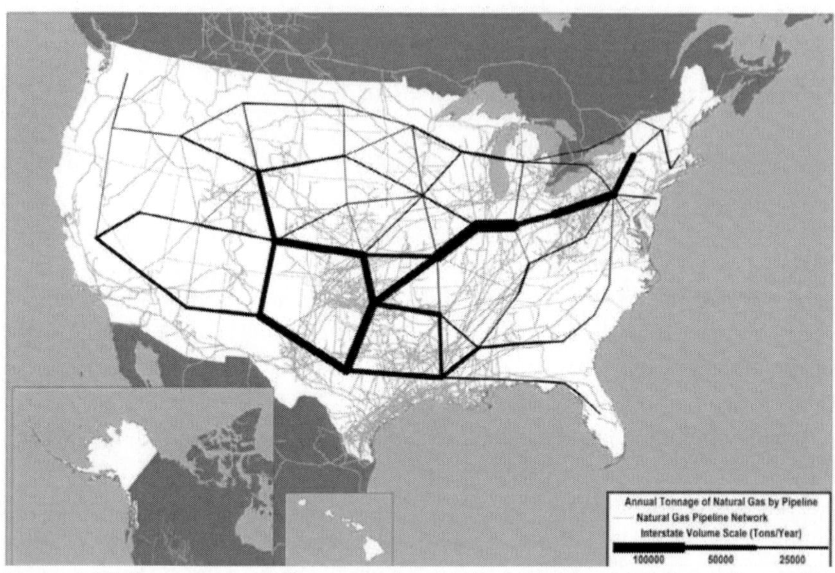

Source: U.S. Department of Transportation, Federal Highway Administration, Office of Freight Management and Operations, Freight Analysis Framework, version 3.4, 2012.

Natural Gas Tonnage Moved by Pipeline: 2007.

Each year, shippers outsource more of their traffic, transportation, and logistics functions to 3PLs, as these companies can offer better purchasing economies, more sophisticated data analysis systems, and better market knowledge than the shipper can afford to develop internally.[115] Many 3PLs describe themselves as the "travel agents" of the freight system, as they are tasked with planning, overseeing, transporting, and storing their clients' goods and products from one end of the supply chain to the other.

There is one notable exception to the general trend toward outsourcing logistics functions, however. Many of the large big-box retailers have developed complex internal logistics operations. They have found that there are economies of scale in their own operations that increase the profitability of maintaining their own warehouses, distribution centers, and trucking fleets.

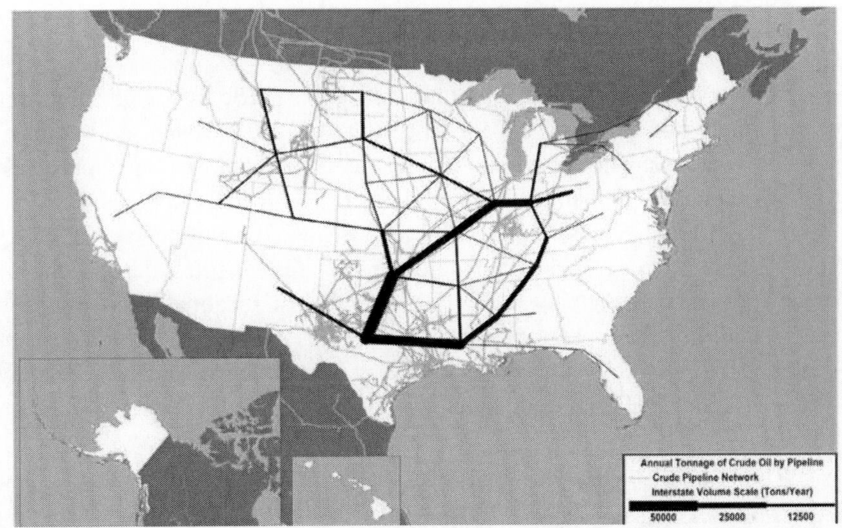

Source: U S. Department of Transportation, Federal Highway Administration, Office of Freight Management and Operations, Freight Analysis Framework, version 3.4, 2012.

Crude Oil Tonnage Moved by Pipeline: 2007.

PIPELINES

Pipelines provide a safe and efficient means of transporting large quantities of energy commodities from wellhead to industry and consumers. Compared to other means of transportation, pipelines offer a capacity and volume advantage, emit few greenhouse gases, and offer an economical way to move energy products over long distances.

History of the Pipeline System

Pipelines have been used for thousands of years. The first application was to transmit drinking water and for irrigation, but 2,500 years ago in China, pipelines were adapted to transport natural gas. This is the first known instance whereby a pipeline transmitted hydrocarbons.

In the United States, pipelines have been used since the late 1700s.[116] Today, there are over 2,600,000 miles of pipelines in the United States—enough to circle the globe about 100 times. Most pipelines are owned by independent pipeline operators, not by oil and gas companies.[117] Pipelines are jointly regulated by the Pipelines and Hazardous Materials Safety Administration (PHMSA) and the Federal Energy Regulatory Commission (FERC).

PHMSA is responsible for ensuring that pipelines are safe, reliable, and environmentally sound and oversees pipeline construction, maintenance, and operation.[118] FERC regulates approval, permitting, and siting for interstate pipelines and sets rates on a pipeline-by-pipeline basis.[119]

Today, the term "pipelines" generally refers to all aspects of the physical infrastructure related to the transmission of energy products. These elements include the pipe and fittings, equipment attached to the pipes, such as valves, compressor units, pump stations, metering stations, and terminals or storage facilities, to name just a few.[120]

Economic Impact of the Pipeline System

Ten percent of the Nation's freight movement, by tonnage, travels through pipelines.[121] Natural gas provides almost 25 percent of the Nation's total energy consumption, and petroleum provides approximately an additional 40 percent of energy consumption. Taken together, pipelines carry nearly two-thirds of the energy used in the United States.[122] These commodities need to be transported quickly and safely, and pipelines move these products efficiently at a high volume.

Pipelines play an important role in ensuring that the Nation's energy commodities are moved quickly, safely, and efficiently, and in so doing, pipelines support the other modes of freight transportation, as well.

RECOMMENDATIONS

Key Recommendations

To safely and efficiently meet the needs of freight movements in the 21st Century, Congress should:

- Direct the Secretary of Transportation, in coordination with the Secretary of the Army and the Commandant of the United States Coast Guard, to establish a comprehensive national freight transportation policy and designate a national, multimodal freight network;
- Ensure robust public investment in all modes of transportation on which freight movement relies, and incentivize additional private investment in freight transportation facilities, to maintain and improve the condition and performance of the freight transportation network;
- Promote and expedite the development and delivery of projects and activities that improve and facilitate the efficient movement of goods;
- Authorize dedicated, sustainable funding for multimodal freight Projects of National and Regional Significance through a grant process and establish clear benchmarks for project selection. Projects eligible for such funding would have a regional or national impact on the overall performance of the multimodal freight network identified by the Secretary of Transportation;
- Direct the Secretary of Transportation, in coordination with the Secretary of the Treasury and the Secretary of the Army, to identify and recommend sustainable sources of revenue across all modes of transportation that would provide the necessary investment in the Nation's multimodal freight network and align contributions with use of, and expected benefit of increased investment in, such network; and
- Review, working through the Committee on Transportation and Infrastructure and the Committee on Ways and Means, the Secretary's freight funding and revenue recommendations and develop specific funding and revenue options for freight transportation projects prior to Congress' consideration of the surface transportation reauthorization bill in 2014.

FUNDING AND FINANCING INVESTMENTS

The United States is at a crossroads. Study after study has indicated that the Nation's infrastructure is crumbling. This deterioration in the condition of the Nation's roadway pavements and bridges can affect the efficiency of goods movement and increase costs associated with freight transportation. Without an increased public and private sector investment in the most critical freight infrastructure facilities, the Nation's long-term economic and business competitiveness will suffer.

While a strong freight transportation network is critical to the Nation's long-term competitiveness, it is well documented that infrastructure investment at all levels of government is insufficient to keep up with operation, maintenance, and capital needs of existing facilities, let alone make investments in critically needed new facilities. Moreover, there is no dedicated source of federal revenue for important multimodal freight projects.

Despite this well documented need for additional infrastructure investment, the Congressional Budget Office projections show that the primary source of federal funding for surface transportation investment — the Highway Trust Fund — will run out of money early in fiscal year 2015. This will require additional revenue be identified to ensure that state and local partners have the resources necessary to maintain existing facilities.

It is important to note that throughout the Panel's deliberations, many of the users of the transportation network — such as truckers, barge operators, manufacturers, and business owners — have expressed a willingness to contribute more to the system, as long as their investment will be used to maintain and upgrade the facilities on which their livelihoods rely.

Surface Transportation Commissions

Congress established the National Surface Transportation Policy and Revenue Study Commission (Policy Commission) in the Safe, Accountable, Flexible, Efficient Transportation Equity Act: A Legacy for Users (SAFETEA-LU), and charged it with forecasting the surface transportation system necessary to support our economy 50 years in the future. The Policy Commission report was issued in January 2008.

The Policy Commission report:

- Identified a significant surface transportation investment gap and called for an annual investment level of between $225 billion and $340 billion—by all levels of government and the private sector—over the next 50 years to upgrade all modes of surface transportation (highways, bridges, public transit, freight rail and intercity passenger rail) to a state of good repair. The current annual capital investment from all government sources in road and bridge infrastructure is $182 billion.
- Proposed that the federal fuel taxes be raised by between 25 cents and 40 cents per gallon to address the funding gap and the rate increase be indexed to the construction cost index and phased in over a period of years.
- Found that the fuel tax would continue to be a viable revenue source for surface transportation at least through 2025. Thereafter, the most promising alternative user fee revenue measure appears to be a vehicle miles traveled (VMT) fee, provided that substantial privacy and collection cost issues can be addressed.
- Called for other user-based fees to be utilized to assist in addressing the shortfall, such as container fees for freight projects and ticket taxes for passenger rail improvements.
- Called for tax policy changes to incentivize expansion of intermodal networks.
- Proposed the expanded use of "congestion pricing" on Federal-aid highways in major metropolitan areas be utilized under conditions that protect the public interest, and restricted the use of revenues generated through congestion pricing to transportation purposes in the travel corridors where the fees are imposed.
- Stipulated that public-private partnerships should be encouraged to attract additional private investment to the surface transportation system, provided that conditions are included to protect the public interest and the movement of interstate commerce.

SAFETEA-LU also created the National Surface Transportation Infrastructure Financing Commission (Financing Commission). The Financing Commission was charged with analyzing future highway and transit needs and the finances of the Highway Trust Fund and making recommendations regarding alternative approaches to financing transportation infrastructure. The Financing Commission's report was issued in February 2009.

The Financing Commission report:

- Found an annual surface transportation investment gap of between $46 billion to $64 billion between 2008 and 2035.
- Concluded that, while there were concerns with the long-term viability of the gas tax, in the near term:
  - The gas tax should be increased by 10 cents per gallon, and indexed to inflation;
  - The diesel tax should be increased 15 cents per gallon, and indexed to inflation;
  - Heavy Vehicle Use Tax (HVUT), which has not been increased since 1983, should be doubled and indexed; and
  - Truck tires excise tax should be indexed to inflation.
- Called for a switch to a more direct form of "user pay" charges over the long-term, specifically calling for the transition to a VMT fee system. Recognizing that the system is not viable in the near term, the report recommended that the transition to such a system be targeted for completion by 2020.
- Recognized the important role innovative financing approaches, such as public-private partnerships and government financial programs, can play as a supplementary source of financing. However, found that these types of financing instruments are heavily dependent on new revenue sources that can be leveraged to repay upfront capital investments.

The Financing Commission report also notes, with regard to proposed National Infrastructure Banks, that any such entity should be structured in a manner that addresses actual funding and credit market gaps and should target assistance to projects that are essential to the national network but that lack access to sufficient resources through existing programs. The report urges Congress to ensure that any such entity is appropriately integrated with or a logical extension of current programs, especially the Transportation Infrastructure Finance and Innovation Act (TIFIA) program. The Financing Commission warns that the potential role of a new infrastructure financing entity should be examined in the context of long-term funding needs and not only as an immediate response to the current disruption in the credit markets.

Freight-Based Financing Options

The reports from the Financing Commission and the Policy Commission discussed potential freight-related charges that could be instituted in the future. Below is a summary the findings on four options to generate revenue to pay for freight-related projects—customs duties and fees, a freight waybill tax, a weight-distance tax, and a container tax.

The Financing Commission evaluated the advantages and disadvantages of each option based on its revenue-raising potential, sustainability, and flexibility; implementation and administration considerations; economic efficiency and impact; equity; and applicability to other levels of government.

Customs Duties and Fees—The Financing Commission found that a portion of the revenues from existing customs duties potentially could be dedicated to transportation infrastructure tied to the movement of those goods—effectively a transfer from the General Fund. While customs duties and fees would be reasonable for a small, dedicated intermodal fund, the large gaps in coverage make it a poor broad-based funding method.

- Allocating a portion of existing customs duties would require no major administrative effort or expansion of legal authority. Alternatively, a transportation use surcharge could be added to the existing customs duty and fee schedule and dedicated to freight transportation infrastructure.
- The Financing Commission found that imposition of a 3.5 percent transportation surcharge would provide approximately $1 billion annually. An increase in the Customs Merchandise Processing Fee by 70 percent would also yield $1 billion annually.
- However, increasing revenues from customs duties and fees may not be consistent with international rules governing trade. Additionally, these fees do not reach the United States exporters who generate much of the local highway use around the port.
- An infrastructure customs fee could be structured to relate to system use (e.g., fee revenues could be dedicated to infrastructure needs at the point they are collected) and could have the benefit of addressing border infrastructure needs that arise from both homeland security and transportation infrastructure requirements that create chokepoints.

Freight Waybill Tax—A freight waybill tax would serve as a sales tax on the shipping costs for freight. Such a tax could be modeled on the aviation system tax, in which passenger and freight users who rely on the same infrastructure and carriers all contribute to fund the system. The air-freight waybill tax currently provides five percent of contributions to the federal Airport and Airway Trust Fund.

- A small percentage tax rate could raise significant revenues with strong sustainability. A 0.1 percent tax on all truck freight waybills would raise about $620 million annually; thus a 0.16 percent rate would raise $1 billion per year.
- A freight waybill tax would be expensive to administer due to the high number of taxpayers and the associated filing, auditing, and enforcement requirements. In addition, the waybill is typically paid by the receiver of goods; however, in some cases it is paid by the benefiting cargo owner outside of the United States Thus, determining how and from whom to collect the tax could be complex.
- Private fleets (e.g., Wal-Mart and Georgia-Pacific) would not be assessed the fee unless waybill-like costs were estimated and imputed to the private company.
- Such a tax would be an indirect user fee, but with less connection to use than the current motor fuel tax (a freight waybill tax generally reflects distance but more heavily equates to the value of the freight).
- While a freight waybill tax would be reasonably equitable, the tax would be related to transportation costs and not system use. In addition, without the implementation of an imputed waybill on captive shippers, the tax would miss as much as one-half of the goods movement industry.
- The Commission found that the process of resolving this gap creates significant implementation and administration costs and would be subject to evasion.

Weight-Distance Tax—Weight-distance taxes are fees imposed on the miles traveled by specific vehicle classes, which take into account the weight and load of a vehicle and essentially impose a premium on heavier vehicles to recover the added wear and tear they cause to the system. This tax can be based on a combination of the actual weight being carried for each trip and the number of miles traveled, on the weight of the truck and the number of axles, or on the average vehicle weight plus load weights. Currently, Oregon,

Kentucky, New Mexico, and New York use state-based variations of the weight-mile tax in combination with a fuel tax (Oregon does not charge a fuel tax for commercial trucks).

- The administrative costs of a weight-distance tax can be high. However, Oregon's tax rates are based on the average weight carried by a vehicle of each class, and, thus, trucking companies only need to keep track of mileage rather than mileage and weight.
- Evasion has been an issue for states with weight-distance taxes (though if states moved to a high-tech system such as Oregon plans to implement, that would cut down on evasion).
- Weight and weight-mile taxes closely correlate system use and costs, including the costs that freight trucks impose on highways. However, these taxes do little to promote targeted investment at key points of the system affecting efficiency (like bottlenecks). Therefore, the Commission found such a tax would be better suited as a funding source for system-wide maintenance.
- Both a weight-only and a weight-distance tax would place a larger tax burden on low-value/high-weight commodities.

Container Tax—A per container fee could be collected at port gates or via a toll collection system in the immediate vicinity of a port and dedicated to an intermodal investment fund. The Port of Long Beach charged container fees to fund the Alameda Corridor project.

- The complexity of actual collection of a national container tax would depend on how the fee is applied. The Commission cautions that duplicative container fees at individual ports coupled with a national fee would be administratively burdensome for shippers and pre-emption of states' ability to impose their own container charge would be problematic as local fees are used to help states fund relief of port congestion.
- A container fee potentially could miss movements at inland waterways and at cross-border or other ports of entry, and it could possibly not account for non-containerized freight movements like bulk cargo. Such a tax could also disadvantage United States ports in competition with those in Mexico and Canada.
- A container tax would be imposed generally on shippers and would not account for non-containerized movements suck as bulk shipments

of commodities or large pieces of equipment like tractors or windmill blades.

- The Commission found that while the container tax is a possibility for funding intermodal projects, its limited coverage makes it a weak option for large-scale funding needs.

Trust Funds

Congress has created four trust funds that collect user fees and disburse revenue for transportation infrastructure, including projects key to freight mobility.

Highway Trust Fund—The Federal-Aid Highway Act of 1956 established the Highway Trust Fund (HTF). The revenues capitalizing the Highway Trust Fund are collected primarily from users of the highway system through federal taxes on fuels and various taxes on trucks.

Since enactment of this legislation, funding from the Highway Trust Fund has been provided to states via formula for the planning and construction of key highway projects that enable the movement of freight. Most highway-related freight projects, as well as some freight rail and freight intermodal projects, are currently eligible to receive funding under one or more existing federal surface transportation programs. Many large freight projects, however, are multimodal in scope, and some aspects of these projects may be ineligible for funding from the HTF. This puts project sponsors in the position of having to cobble together funding for large multimodal freight projects from a variety of different sources.

The HTF is also facing a significant revenue shortfall, raising questions about the ability of the HTF to sustain current investment levels. In recent years, outlays from the HTF have been significantly greater than the amount of revenues collected in highway user fee revenues. As a result, between fiscal year 2008 and fiscal year 2014, Congress has transferred approximately $54 billion from the General Fund to maintain the solvency of the HTF. This HTF solvency issue is expected to continue, with the Congressional Budget Office projecting that the HTF will face a cash deficit of $132 billion over fiscal year 2012 to fiscal year 2023.

Harbor Maintenance Trust Fund—The harbor maintenance tax (HMT) is an existing revenue mechanism that supports the federal Harbor

Maintenance Trust Fund (HMTF) through an ad valorem tax on the value of passenger tickets and declared commercial cargo loaded onto or unloaded from vessels using federally maintained harbors. The HMT is assessed at a rate of 0.125 percent of cargo value ($1.25 per $1,000 in cargo value). The HMT could be increased and dedicated to an intermodal investment fund (or existing revenues from the tax could be redirected to such a fund). In recent years, HMTF annual expenditures appropriated for harbor maintenance have remained relatively flat.

- While increasing the HMT would not require major administrative effort or expansion of legal authority, the portion of the tax imposed on imports could create issues with international rules governing trade (similar to issues associated with increasing customs duties and fees). Additionally, the HMT does not reach the United States exporters who generate much of the local highway use around ports.
- An HMT increase could be structured to relate to system use if the proceeds were dedicated to infrastructure needs at or near ports of entry, particularly seaports. In this case, there would be relatively high geographic equity and a reasonable level of user equity if funding were spent on infrastructure to support ports.

Inland Waterways Trust Fund—The Inland Waterways Trust Fund (IWTF) is capitalized by a fuel tax on commercial barges and cost-sharing requirements for inland waterway projects. From 1986 to today, the balance in the IWTF has varied considerably. Beginning in 1992, balances increased reaching their highest level in 2002 at $413 million. Beginning in 2005, expenditures began to outpace collections and concurrently several projects far exceeded their original cost estimates and balances dropped sharply. Significant concerns have been raised as to the economic viability of the IWTF under the present fuel tax approach.

Airport and Airway Trust Fund—The Airport and Airway Trust Fund (AATF) provides dedicated funding for the Nation's aviation system, including air freight functions. Revenues are derived from aviation-related excise taxes on passengers, cargo, and fuel and in turn provide funding for capital improvements to United States airports.

Transportation Investment Generating Economic Recovery (TIGER) and Projects of National and Regional Significance (PNRS)

The Transportation Investment Generating Economic Recovery (TIGER) discretionary grant program is funded through the General Fund of the Treasury and administered by the Department of Transportation (DOT). The TIGER program was originally created as part of the American Recovery and Reinvestment Act of 2009 and is a competitive grant program whereby DOT distributes appropriated funds for transportation infrastructure projects around the Nation. The TIGER program has been funded every year since its inception in 2009.

Under DOT's TIGER grants, many freight projects have successfully received funding. However, due to the demand and structural limitations of the TIGER program as well as the large expense of many key freight transportation facilities, the dollar amount of each grant under TIGER is generally insufficient to fund individual freight projects in significant measure. As such, the TIGER program is helpful in bringing freight projects online, but without additional resources is insufficient as a means of funding for such facilities, in and of itself.

Similar in many ways to the TIGER program is the Projects of National and Regional Significance (PNRS) program authorized by Congress in SAFETEA-LU and reauthorized in the Moving Ahead for Progress in the 21st Century Act (MAP-21). This program provides competitive grant funding for high-cost surface transportation projects that provide significant national and regional economic benefits and increase global competitiveness. MAP-21 authorized $500 million for the PNRS program from the General Fund for fiscal year 2013. As such, the PNRS program is subject to annual appropriations and has not yet received funding.

Transportation Infrastructure Finance and Innovation Act (TIFIA)

Another tool that project sponsors have in funding large-scale infrastructure projects is the Transportation Infrastructure Finance and Innovation Act (TIFIA) program, which is capitalized at $1 billion in fiscal year 2014. The TIFIA program provides federal credit assistance to project sponsors through low interest-rate loans. Through participation in the TIFIA program, federal funds can be leveraged to provide greater purchasing power for large transportation facilities.

Railroad Rehabilitation & Improvement Financing (RRIF)

The Railroad Rehabilitation & Improvement Financing (RRIF) program was originally established by the Transportation Equity Act for the 21st Century (TEA-21), and later amended by SAFETEA-LU. Under this program, the Federal Railroad Administration is authorized to provide direct loans and loan guarantees up to $35 billion to finance development of railroad infrastructure. The funding may be used to (1) acquire, improve, or rehabilitate intermodal or rail equipment or facilities, including track, components of track, bridges, yards, buildings and shops; (2) refinance outstanding debt incurred for acquisition, improvement, or rehabilitation of rail equipment or facilities; and (3) develop or establish new intermodal or railroad facilities. Eligible applicants include railroads, state and local governments, government-sponsored authorities and corporations, joint ventures that include at least one railroad, and limited option freight shippers who intend to construct a new rail connection. Direct loans can fund up to 100 percent of a railroad project with repayment periods of up to 35 years and interest rates equal to the federal government's cost of borrowing.

State Transportation Funding Packages

Many states are also faced with inadequate funding to address their transportation needs. As a result, states such as Virginia, Maryland, Wyoming, Arkansas, and Vermont have recently passed measures to increase state revenue for transportation projects.

For instance, in May 2013, Virginia Governor Bob McDonnell signed a statewide transportation funding plan that he had worked with the state legislature to develop. The proposal, HB 2313, "Virginia's Road to the Future", raises revenue through a variety of sources including: eliminating the excise taxes on gasoline and diesel and replacing them with sales taxes on gasoline and diesel; increasing the state sales tax; and imposing a fee on alternative fuel vehicles.

The plan is expected to provide approximately $6 billion in additional transportation funding (more than $3.4 billion in additional statewide transportation funding, more than $1.5 billion in additional funding for Northern Virginia, and more than $1 billion in additional funding for Hampton Roads) over the next five years.

Public-Private Partnerships (PPPs)

In addition to the public grant funding, individual states have begun using public-private partnerships (PPPs) to stretch governmental contributions to large freight transportation projects. A recent PPP at the Port of Baltimore provides a prime example of a freight transportation facility that was brought online as a result of cooperative planning and development between private industry and governmental entities.

In January 2010, the Maryland Port Administration and a private port operator entered a 50-year lease and concession agreement for the Seagirt Marine Terminal at the Port of Baltimore. Under the agreement, the port operator is responsible for daily operations and the construction of a new 50-foot berth, including four ship-to-shore cranes.

The port operator will also make hundreds of millions of dollars of capital improvements to the terminal. After making an annual payment to the Maryland Port Authority, the port operator will receive the net revenues from the business developed by the expanded terminal facility.

To safely and efficiently meet the needs of freight movements in the 21st Century, Congress should:

- Ensure robust public investment in all modes of transportation on which freight movement relies, and incentivize additional private investment in freight transportation facilities, to maintain and improve the condition and performance of the freight transportation network.
- Direct the Secretary of Transportation, in coordination with the Secretary of the Treasury and the Secretary of the Army, to identify and recommend sustainable sources of revenue across all modes of transportation that would provide the necessary investment in the Nation's multimodal freight network and align contributions with use of, and expected benefit of increased investment in, such network.

- Review, working through the Committee on Transportation and Infrastructure and the Committee on Ways and Means, the Secretary's freight funding and revenue recommendations and develop specific funding and revenue options for freight transportation projects prior to Congress' consideration of the surface transportation reauthorization bill in 2014.
- Authorize dedicated, sustainable funding for multimodal freight Projects of National and Regional Significance through a grant process and establish clear benchmarks for project selection. Projects eligible for such funding would have a regional or national impact on the overall performance of the multimodal freight network identified by the Secretary of Transportation.
- Encourage public-private partnerships and the use of innovative financing for freight projects.

PLANNING AND PROJECT DELIVERY

Planning and project delivery are key to any functioning transportation system. Many governmental and non-governmental entities are involved in this process. When it comes to the planning and delivery of large freight projects with regional or national importance, this process becomes more complicated and important because it can involve multiple jurisdictions and require significant coordination among various entities.

Transportation Planning Process

Generally, state departments of transportation, metropolitan planning organizations (MPOs), and rural planning commissions work together to create a statewide transportation improvement plan (STIP) listing all of the surface transportation projects that are eligible for funding. In addition to the STIP, these organizations may also work together to create a long-range transportation improvement plan with proposals for future consideration.

The Moving Ahead for Progress in the 21st Century Act created a new apportionment for metropolitan planning. Prior to MAP-21, metropolitan planning activities were funded as a set-aside from the formula programs. Under MAP-21, states are required to use funds under this program for statewide and nonmetropolitan transportation planning activities and are required to make funds available to MPOs for metropolitan transportation planning activities. The amount of funds allocated to each MPO within a state is determined by a number of factors, including population, air quality, status of transportation planning, and transportation needs of the metropolitan area.

Planning Freight Projects

While the general transportation planning process is the same for projects that directly impact freight movement and those that do not, freight projects often have difficulty competing with other projects. There are a number of possible reasons for this difficulty, including difficulty accounting for the public benefits of these projects and concerns over providing funding from one jurisdiction for projects that may primarily benefit another jurisdiction. Large freight projects often add additional layers of complexity. Many freight projects are located in urban areas, and city governments or port authorities often take a leading role in developing plans for these projects. Furthermore, freight projects often cross state boundaries, implicating multiple state departments of transportation and MPOs. Given that planning bodies are responsible for focusing on the needs and issues of their specific jurisdiction, planning for and advancing multi-jurisdictional projects requires significant coordination.

Project Delivery

The environmental review process required under the National Environmental Policy Act (NEPA) is designed to bring all the relevant interested parties into the process so that their concerns will be considered adequately throughout the review. The process applies to projects being advanced with environmental impact statements, and can be applied, at the discretion of the Secretary of Transportation, to projects being advanced with other environmental documents. As the lead agency, DOT is responsible for defining the project's purpose and need, after public comments and interagency participation. DOT is also responsible for developing a range of alternatives to be considered for the project.

Completing a major highway project can take 15 years, but only a fraction of that time involves actual construction. MAP-21 streamlined this review process for highway projects by requiring the Secretary to set deadlines to make sure all environmental approvals occur within four years, by providing categorical exclusions to the environmental review process for certain projects that meet specific criteria, and by requiring the Comptroller General to conduct a study on which state laws and procedures provide the same level of environmental protection as Federal law. This process does not apply to other modes of transportation.

Case Study: CREATE Project

Chicago is the largest freight rail hub in North America. Today, six of the seven Class I railroads converge in the region, accounting for the movement of approximately one quarter of all United States freight rail traffic and one-half of all United States intermodal rail traffic. Chicago's antiquated rail infrastructure has led it to become the largest United States freight rail chokepoint.

To help mitigate the rail-related congestion in the Chicago region and meet the future demand for freight rail service across the country, the Chicago Region Environmental and Transportation Efficiency Program (CREATE) was created ten years ago as a public-private partnership between the Chicago Department of Transportation, Illinois Department of Transportation, freight railroads, United States Department of Transportation, Metra, and Amtrak to help mitigate the rail-related congestion in the Chicago region. CREATE consists of 70 individual projects including 25 highway-rail grade separations, six passenger-freight rail grade separations, rail infrastructure improvements, technology upgrades, viaduct improvements, grade crossing safety enhancements, and signalization.

As of May 2013, there were 17 projects completed, 11 projects under construction, 21 projects in design and environmental review, and 21 projects yet to begin. To date, over $1.2 billion has been committed to CREATE, but the total estimated cost for completion is $3.3 billion. When complete, CREATE will enhance passenger rail service, reduce motorist delays, increase public safety, improve air quality, create and retain jobs, and strengthen economic competitiveness. CREATE demonstrates how many organizations and interest groups can come together to effectively plan and fund a large freight project that will improve the efficiency, safety, and performance of the freight system in the region and across the Nation.

To safely and efficiently meet the needs of freight movements in the 21st Century, Congress should:

- Direct the Secretary of Transportation, in coordination with the Secretary of the Army and the Commandant of the United States Coast Guard, to establish a comprehensive national freight transportation policy and designate a national, multimodal freight network.
- Prioritize solutions to modernize infrastructure and utilize technology to reduce congestion to improve the flow of freight.
- Require metropolitan and statewide planning agencies to consider the supply chain, freight movement, and regional and national freight priorities when setting short-and long-range goals and when developing transportation improvement plans.
- Require metropolitan and statewide planning agencies to solicit the participation of freight industry professionals and affected communities when setting short-and long-range goals and when developing transportation improvement plans.
- Require the Secretary of Transportation to identify corridor-based solutions to freight mobility, taking into account the Nation's entire transportation network.
- Require critical freight infrastructure owners and operators to develop cyber vulnerability assessments and cyber incident response plans, as part of existing sector-specific security assessments and plans required by the Department of Homeland Security. For ports, these assessments should be done as part of the assessments required under 46 U.S.C. 70102, and these plans should be done as part of the plans required under 46 U.S.C. 70103.
- Establish policies and set benchmarks to accelerate the transition from project development to construction for freight projects.
- Identify and encourage the use of low-cost measures to alleviate highway congestion.
- Direct the Secretary of Transportation to promulgate the rulemaking required under 23 U.S.C. 150(c), establishing performance measures by which States can assess the quality of freight movement on the Interstate System.

- Direct the Secretary of Transportation to identify performance goals and performance measures by which States can assess the quality of freight movement across all modes of transportation.
- Cut red tape and encourage the Secretary of Transportation to streamline project delivery across all modes of transportation.

HIGHWAYS AND TRUCKING

As discussed above, the Highway Trust Fund faces pending insolvency. Without new revenue, the Trust Fund will be unable to provide states with necessary resources to maintain and improve the Federal-aid Highway System. The condition of roadway pavements and bridges can affect the efficiency of goods movement and increase costs associated with freight transportation. Highways are key to the Nation's freight network, because almost all consumer goods travel on the highway system for some portion of the journey.

To safely and efficiently meet the needs of freight movements in the 21st Century, Congress should:

- Ensure that states have the resources necessary to maintain and improve freight movement on Federal-aid Highways by addressing the looming shortfall in the Highway Trust Fund with sustainable revenue.
- Encourage the Secretary of Transportation to complete the Comprehensive Truck Size and Weight Limits Study conducted in accordance with section 32801 of the Moving Ahead for Progress in the 21st Century Act as thoroughly and judiciously as possible.
- Direct the Secretary of Transportation to determine whether the definition of the primary highway freight network pursuant to 23 U.S.C. 167 is sufficient to address the national highway freight network.
- Encourage states, localities, and the private sector to designate resources for commercial driver training to be made available to all organizations that provide such training.

Section 1115 of MAP-21 required the Secretary of Transportation to designate a primary highway freight network of 27,000 centerline miles. The purpose of this network is to identify the infrastructure facilities that are most important to the movement of freight on the Nation's highways. Final designation of the primary freight network is due imminently.

FREIGHT RAIL

Freight rail provides efficient long-haul and short-haul service and integrates closely with the trucking industry. Because the freight railroads are private entities, they own the infrastructure over which they operate, meaning they also invest heavily in those networks. In 2011, the freight railroads invested over $23 billion in capital expenditures to improve and expand their networks. The RRIF loan program is a vehicle that the federal government can use to leverage this private investment and deliver projects that are key for intermodal freight mobility.

Positive Train Control (PTC) refers to the technologies designed to stop or slow a train automatically before certain accidents that are caused by human error can occur. PTC is statutorily required to be installed by the end of 2015 for certain routes. For a variety of reasons, PTC is an unprecedented technology challenge. Freight railroads have already invested billions of dollars to meet this deadline, but there are many technological and non-technological barriers that remain.

To safely and efficiently meet the needs of freight movements in the 21st Century, Congress should:

- Encourage adequate investment in rail corridor projects that facilitate freight movement.
- Direct the Secretary of Transportation to conduct stronger outreach to freight railroads about the potential benefits of the Railroad Rehabilitation and Improvement Financing (RRIF) loan program, and improve the process for approving applications.
- Work with the Secretary of Transportation, freight and passenger railroads, commuter railroads, railroad employee representatives, and other interested parties to evaluate proposals to extend the deadline for installation of Positive Train Control regulations, mandated pursuant to the Rail Safety Improvement Act of 2008 (P.L. 110-432).

SHIPPING AND PORTS

As discussed above, the Harbor Maintenance Trust Fund maintains a positive balance, yet there is still a large backlog of maritime infrastructure projects that need to be completed.

Wisely utilizing existing revenues is the first step toward improving the efficiency and reliability of this critical aspect of the Nation's freight system.

To safely and efficiently meet the needs of freight movements in the 21st Century, Congress should:

- Appropriate funds annually from the Harbor Maintenance Trust Fund in an amount equal to the revenue collected by the Trust Fund.
- Draw down the $7 billion balance of the Harbor Maintenance Trust Fund, without adversely affecting appropriations for other programs, projects, and activities carried out by the Corps of Engineers for other authorized purposes.
- Expand eligible uses of Harbor Maintenance Trust Fund expenditures to include other activities in the water that are adjacent to navigation channels.
- Direct the Secretary of the Army, in consultation with the Secretary of Transportation and the Commandant of the United States Coast Guard, to prioritize maritime development projects, including port deepening projects, in the Corps of Engineer's annual budget submission.
- Encourage the full utilization of marine highways to expand the capacity of the freight transportation network, alleviate surface transportation congestion, and ensure the reliable movement of freight via short sea shipping.
- Direct the Secretary of Transportation, in coordination with the Secretary of the Treasury and the Secretary of the Army, to study the degree to which shippers, seeking to avoid payment of the Harbor Maintenance Tax, divert cargo bound for the United States from the Nation's ports. This study should expand upon the July 2012 study conducted by the Federal Maritime Commission.
- Encourage ports and intermodal facilities to maximize efficiency through off-peak cargo movement.

- Encourage, coordinate, and support navigation technology research, development, and investment to improve navigation safety and efficiency and reduce the risk of accidents and disruption of the freight network.

INLAND WATERWAYS

Inland waterways are vitally important to the health of the Nation's economy. It is estimated that without the barges and towboats operating on the inland waterways, the Nation would need 6.3 million railroad cars or 25 million trucks to haul the difference.

However, much of the critical infrastructure for waterborne transportation is in dire need of repair. More than one-half of the locks and dams in the United States are over 50 years old.

To safely and efficiently meet the needs of freight movements in the 21st Century, Congress should:

- Authorize adequate funding for operations and maintenance of the Nation's inland waterways system.
- Direct the Secretary of the Army, in coordination with the Secretary of the Treasury, to assess financing options for the inland waterways system.
- Work with the Inland Waterways User Board, states, and other interested parties to plan and prioritize federal investment in the inland waterways system.

AIR CARGO

Air cargo is the fastest way to ship goods over long distances, and air freight is high value cargo. Less than three percent of total freight by weight ships by air, but this represents over $6.4 trillion worth of goods per year, which is nearly 35 percent of all freight value. Today, the Federal Aviation Administration (FAA) is responsible for ensuring the safe navigation of aircraft within the Nation's airspace.

However, the basic elements of the FAA system have not changed significantly in over 60 years. The Next Generation Air Transportation System (NextGen) is FAA's solution, employing new technology, modernized procedures, and resulting in added capacity, increased productivity, and greater safety.

To safely and efficiently meet the needs of freight movements in the 21st Century, Congress should:

- Authorize adequate funding and programmatic support to implement new air traffic control technologies and operational capabilities to facilitate the transition to the Next Generation Air Transportation System supporting the Nation's air freight system.

APPENDIX A. PANEL SCOPE OF WORK

Committee on Transportation and Infrastructure
U.S. House of Representatives
Washington, DC 20515

Bill Shuster
Chairman

Nick J. Rahall, II
Ranking Member

April 23, 2013

Dear Panel Member:

We write to notify you that you have been selected to serve on a panel on freight transportation constituted under the Rules of the Committee on Transportation and Infrastructure. The panel has been tasked to examine the current state of freight transportation in the United States and how improving freight transportation can strengthen the United States economy.

The panel will recommend ways to improve the movement of freight across all modes of the Nation's transportation network. The panel will report its findings, including any recommendations for possible legislation, to the Full Committee.

Panel Name:

Panel on 21st Century Freight Transportation

Panel Members:

John J. Duncan, Jr., TN, Chairman
Gary Miller, CA
Rick Crawford, AR
Richard Hanna, NY
Daniel Webster, FL
Markwayne Mullin, OK

Jerrold Nadler, NY, Ranking Member
Corrine Brown, FL
Daniel Lipinski, IL
Albio Sires, NJ
Janice Hahn, CA

Rules and Procedures:

The panel is constituted under Rule XVIII of the Rules of the Committee on Transportation and Infrastructure to serve for a period of six months beginning on the date of its organization, April 24, 2013.

The panel will follow the rules and procedures of the Committee on Transportation and Infrastructure, as adopted by the Committee for the 113th Congress, in all of its meetings, hearings, and other activities. These rules and procedures include the meeting, hearing, quorum, and record vote requirements of Committee rules.

Staffing:

The panel will be assisted by staff of the House Committee on Transportation and Infrastructure designated by the Chairman and Ranking Member of the Committee for this purpose.

Work Plan:

The panel will examine the current state of freight transportation in the United States to identify (1) the role freight transportation plays in the U.S. economy; (2) ways to increase the efficiency, safety, and overall condition and performance of the Nation's freight network; (3) how technology assists in the movement of freight; and (4) financing options for transportation projects that improve freight mobility.

In examining the Nation's freight mobility issues, the panel will focus on four primary areas:

- The role freight transportation plays in the U.S. economy—
  - What are the economic impacts of inefficiencies in our Nation's freight transportation network?
  - How does the transportation of freight impact consumers?
  - How do changes in the business models and the global supply chain impact our freight transportation network and the U.S. economy?
  - How does U.S. transportation and infrastructure policy affect global supply chains and the Nation's global competitiveness?

- Ways to increase the efficiency, safety, and overall performance of the Nation's freight network—
  - What are the sources of inefficiencies in our Nation's freight transportation network?
  - How can the efficient movement of goods between highways, ports, inland waterways, railroads, air carriers, and pipelines be improved?
  - Are states, localities, and the Federal government adequately considering freight transportation as they plan and select transportation projects?
  - How can the safety of freight movement across all modes be improved?

- How technology assists in the movement of freight—
  - What role does technology play in transporting freight?
  - How can freight transportation better utilize technology to improve efficiency, safety, and performance?
  - What are the cybersecurity vulnerabilities for freight critical infrastructure, such as intelligent transportation systems, railway signals, the air traffic control system, and the Next Generation Air Transportation System?
  - What safeguards are necessary to protect the cybersecurity of freight critical infrastructure and ensure the safe and efficient movement of freight?

- More efficient uses of Federal dollars to fund transportation projects that improve freight mobility—
  - What role should states, localities, and the Federal government play in funding or financing projects that facilitate the movement of freight?
  - What role should the private sector play in funding or financing projects that facilitate the movement of freight?
  - What are the financing or funding options for projects that promote efficient movement of goods between modes of transportation or that involve large multi-state freight projects?
  - What are the effects of different financing or funding options on shippers, carriers, and consumers?

If you or your staff have any questions or need further information, please contact the Committee office at (202) 225-9446.

Sincerely,

Bill Shuster
Chairman

Nick J. Rahall, II
Ranking Member

APPENDIX B. PANEL ACTIVITIES

Date	Title
April 24, 2013	Hearing – "Overview of the United States' Freight Transportation System"
May 15, 2013	Roundtable Policy Discussion – "Coordinating Federal Efforts to Improve Freight Transportation"
May 28, 2013 to May 31, 2013	Site Visit – Southern California
May 29, 2013	Roundtable Policy Discussion – "Navigating the Complexities of America's Largest Port Facilities"
May 30, 2013	Hearing – "How Southern California Freight Transportation Challenges Impact the Nation"
June 20, 2013 to June 21, 2013	Site Visit – Memphis Region
June 26, 2013	Hearing – "How Logistics Facilitate an Efficient Freight Transportation System"
July 17, 2013	Roundtable Policy Discussion – "Effectively Coordinating Freight Planning Activities"
July 25, 2013 to July 27, 2013	Site Visit – New York City Region
July 26, 2013	Hearing – "How Freight Transportation Challenges in Urban Areas Impact the Nation"
August 22, 2013 to August 23, 2013	Site Visit – Norfolk, Virginia
October 1, 2013	Hearing – "Perspectives from Users of the Nation's Freight System"
October 10, 2013	Hearing – "Funding the Nation's Freight System"

APPENDIX C. SUMMARY OF HEARING – "OVERVIEW OF THE UNITED STATES' FREIGHT TRANSPORTATION SYSTEM"

Overview

The Panel on 21st Century Freight Transportation met on Wednesday, April 24, 2013, at 10:00 a.m., in 2167 Rayburn House Office Building to receive testimony related to the importance of freight transportation to the United States economy. At this hearing, the Panel received testimony on the current operation of the freight network, what challenges impact its performance, and what can be done to improve the efficiency and safety of freight transportation.

Points of Discussion

- The Nation's freight transportation network affects the day-to-day lives of every citizen, and given its multimodal nature, the system as a whole and how its parts work together need to be examined and improved for future capacity and demand.
- As an essential part of the Nation's freight network, the highway system moves approximately 50 percent of all freight moved in the United States via trucking. Unfortunately, the negative impacts of congestion slow the efficiency of the highway system as a reliable freight mode.
- Carrying more freight than any other mode of surface transportation over long distances, railroads carry 43 percent of intercity freight and are continually working to improve and expand their networks.
- With respect to ports and maritime freight movement, cargo ships move 75 percent of international freight every year by water. To continue efficiently exporting such a large volume of goods, investment is necessary in port infrastructure and land-side connections.

- Air cargo carriers play a large role in transporting goods in both domestic and international supply chains, moving cargo quickly and often moving goods of high value.
- As the safest and most efficient way to transport hazardous materials, pipelines play an important role in delivering crucial products such as natural gas throughout the country.

Witnesses

Fred Smith, Chairman, President, and Chief Executive Officer
FedEx Corporation

Charles W. Moorman, Chairman, President, and Chief Executive Officer
Norfolk Southern Corporation

James Newsome, President and Chief Executive Officer
South Carolina Ports Authority

Derek Leathers, President
Werner Enterprises

Edward Wytkind, President, Transportation Trades Department
AFL-CIO

APPENDIX D. SUMMARY OF HEARING – "HOW SOUTHERN CALIFORNIA FREIGHT TRANSPORTATION CHALLENGES IMPACT THE NATION"

Overview

The Panel on 21st Century Freight Transportation met on Thursday, May 30, 2013 at the historic Santa Fe Depot located at 1170 West 3rd Street, San Bernardino, California, to receive testimony related to ways the freight challenges of Southern California impact the Nation. During this hearing, the Panel received testimony on the current operation of the freight network in Southern California, the unique challenges that impact its performance, and how these issues resonate throughout the country and impact the freight system as a whole.

Points of Discussion

- The multimodal Southern California freight system is one of the most important gateways in the entire country, incorporating ports, international border crossings, highways, railways, and air cargo facilities. Creating 60,000 local jobs, the freight industry in Southern California brings in over $30 billion in local, state, and federal tax revenue yearly.
- Southern California ranks as the third-largest manufacturing region in the Nation.
- Congestion, bottlenecks, and other inefficiencies hinder the Southern California region's ability to import and move goods throughout the Nation, increasing costs and transit times.
- Given the connected nature of the Nation's supply chain, the issues impacting this region's freight system have a direct and tangible impact on the economic competitiveness of states thousands of miles away.

Witnesses

Kome Ajise, Deputy Director for Planning and Modal Programs
California Department of Transportation

Hasan Ikhrata, Executive Director
Southern California Association of Governments

Marnie O'Brien Primmer, Executive Director
Mobility 21

Scott Moore, Vice President for Public Affairs
Union Pacific

Mike Fox, President and Chief Executive Officer
Fox Transportation

Rick Richmond, Former Chief Executive Officer
Alameda Corridor-East Construction Authority

APPENDIX E. SUMMARY OF HEARING – "HOW LOGISTICS FACILITATE AN EFFICIENT FREIGHT TRANSPORTATION SYSTEM"

Overview

The Panel on 21st Century Freight Transportation met on Wednesday, June 26, 2013 at 1:00 p.m. in 2167 Rayburn House Office Building to receive testimony related to the impact of the logistics industry on the United States freight network. During the hearing, the Panel received testimony concerning the correlation between logistics and a productive, efficient, and safe national freight system and suggestions to strengthen this relationship.

Points of Discussion

- The logistics industry is one of the most valuable parts of the Nation's freight system because it improves the efficiency of the supply chain.
- Logistics providers play a key role in alleviating inefficiencies and bottlenecks, which impede freight mobility and drive up the cost of goods.
- Manufacturers and retailers can maximize the value of third-party logistics by using the concept of Just-in-Time Delivery, minimizing carrying costs and increasing business efficiency.

Witnesses

David Abney, Chief Operating Officer
United Parcel Service

Tracy Rosser, Senior Vice President, Transportation
Walmart Corporation

Scott Satterlee, Senior Vice President, Transportation
C.H. Robinson

Mark DeFabis, President and Chief Executive Officer
International Development Systems

Richard Fisher, President
Falcon Global Edge

Ed Hamberger, President and Chief Executive Officer
Association of American Railroads

APPENDIX F. SUMMARY OF HEARING – "HOW FREIGHT TRANSPORTATION CHALLENGES IN URBAN AREAS IMPACT THE NATION"

Overview

The Panel on 21st Century Freight Transportation met on Friday, July 26, 2013 at 1:30 p.m. at the Alexander Hamilton United States Custom House, located at One Bowling Green, New York, New York. The Panel received testimony related to the ways in which urban freight challenges impact the Nation. During this hearing, the Panel received testimony concerning the operation of the freight network in urban areas, the unique challenges that impact performance in these areas, and how these issues impact the rest of the Nation's freight system.

Points of Discussion

- Freight transportation in urban areas is complex and sensitive, and mitigated by several dueling factors. Given the interconnected nature of the Nation's freight transportation system, issues that impact one region of the country inevitably have a ripple effect throughout the entire network.

- Congestion remains one of the most costly hurdles for urban area freight transportation. Congestion, by increasing transit times, increases the cost of goods for consumers.
- State transportation departments and metropolitan planning organizations generally work together to create a long term strategy for urban freight planning. However, freight projects that cross state lines often have difficulty competing in a state-based formula program. Planning and advocating for multi-jurisdictional projects require significant coordination amongst several groups.
- The New York City metropolitan area experiences some of the most critical freight challenges of any region in the country, particularly the ability to move goods efficiently across the Hudson River. Without a viable alternative, trucking across ageing and congested infrastructure is the best option to move goods throughout the region.

Witnesses

Patrick Foye, Executive Director
Port Authority of New York and New Jersey

William Flynn, President and Chief Executive Officer
Atlas Air Worldwide Holdings

Gerry Coyle, Vice President for Environmental & Sustainability
Evans Network

William Goetz, Resident Vice President for New York City, New Jersey, and Philadelphia
CSX Transportation

Appendix G. Summary of Hearing – "Perspectives from Users of the Nation's Freight System"

Overview

The Panel on 21st Century Freight Transportation met on Tuesday, October 1, 2013, at 2:00 p.m., in 2167 Rayburn House Office Building to receive testimony related to the ways in which the agriculture and manufacturing industries rely on the Nation's freight transportation system to remain competitive. At this hearing, the Panel received testimony on the specific freight transportation needs of these industries and the impact that the level of performance of the freight system has on the ability of these industries to remain competitive.

Points of Discussion

- Depending on the particularities of the goods being produced, manufacturers often have unique freight transportation needs. The sophistication and efficiency of the Nation's freight system allow for manufacturers to deliver goods in a way that supports the competitiveness of the industry. However, more investment is needed to support growth.
- The manufacturing and agriculture industries are concerned that the Nation's current failure to adequately invest in infrastructure will cede past gains to global competitors, especially in the agriculture industry.
- Aside from general issues related to the market for agricultural commodities, transportation costs are the most significant factor impacting the bottom line for farmers and other participants in the agriculture industry.

Witnesses

Tom Kadien, Senior Vice President, Consumer Packaging
International Paper

F. Edmond Johnston, III, Sustainability Manager
DuPont

William Roberson, Materials & Logistics Manager
Nucor Steel Berkeley

Bill J. Reed, Vice President, Public Affairs
Riceland Foods, Inc.

Appendix H. Summary of Hearing – "Funding the Nation's Freight System"

Overview

The Panel on 21st Century Freight Transportation met on Thursday, October 10, 2013, at 1:00 p.m., in 2167 Rayburn House Office Building to receive testimony related to the ways in which freight projects can be funded. At this hearing, the Panel received testimony on the various proposals on ways to raise new revenue and use existing revenue more wisely in the funding of freight infrastructure projects across the Nation.

Points of Discussion

- Most highway-related freight projects, as well as some freight rail and freight intermodal projects, are currently eligible to receive funding under one or more existing federal surface transportation programs. Many large freight projects, however, are multimodal in scope, and some aspects of these projects may be ineligible for funding from the Highway Trust Fund. Freight projects that cross state lines often have difficulty competing in a state-based highway formula program. Freight projects also receive federal assistance through the Harbor Maintenance Trust Fund, the Transportation Investment Generating Economic Recovery grants, and Transportation Infrastructure Finance and Innovation Act grants.
- Freight infrastructure facilities are in need of upgrading and current federal funding available for freight projects still leaves states with unmet needs. Additional federal resources are needed to address the Nation's freight transportation needs.
- Some states have recently passed measures to increase state revenue for transportation projects. States have also explored public-private partnerships to fund freight projects.

Witnesses

The Honorable Sean T. Connaughton, Secretary
Virginia Department of Transportation

Leif Dormsjo, Deputy Secretary
Maryland Department of Transportation

Robert D. Atkinson, President
Information Technology and Innovation Foundation

Jack L. Schenendorf, Of Counsel
Covington & Burling, LLP

David Seltzer, Co-Founder
Mercator Advisors

APPENDIX I. SUMMARY OF SITE VISIT – SOUTHERN CALIFORNIA

Overview

In order to gain a better understanding of freight movement in the region and to hear from local stakeholders, members and staff of the Panel on 21st Century Freight Transportation traveled to different areas of Southern California from Tuesday, May 28 to Friday, May 31, 2013.

Sites Visited

- On Tuesday, May 28, 2013, Members and staff received a briefing on the cargo operations at Los Angeles International Airport, and then toured the cargo operations of the Mercury Air Group. Later in the day, they met with officials from the Los Angeles Metropolitan Transportation Authority.
- On Wednesday, May 29, 2013, Members and staff received a briefing on port operations from officials of the Port of Los Angeles and Port

of Long Beach; toured the International Transportation Services Terminal and the Middle Harbor Redevelopment Project at the Port of Long Beach; toured the Port of Los Angeles and the Port of Long Beach by boat, accompanied by officials from both ports and local freight stakeholders; and Members held a roundtable discussion with industry stakeholders on port operations at the APM Terminal.

- On Thursday, May 30, 2013, Members and staff traveled on BNSF rail cars up the Alameda Corridor to the intermodal rail yard in Hobart, and out the Alameda Corridor East towards San Bernardino. Members and staff received briefings on the facilities en route by BNSF senior officers and local stakeholders. Upon arriving in San Bernardino, Members and staff visited the BNSF San Bernardino Rail Yard. Members held a field hearing entitled "How Southern California Freight Transportation Challenges Impact the Nation."

APPENDIX J. SUMMARY OF SITE VISIT – MEMPHIS REGION

Overview

On Thursday, June 20 and Friday, June 21, 2013, Members and staff of the Panel on 21st Century Freight Transportation traveled to the Memphis region for a series of site visits, meetings, and a working lunch discussion.

Sites Visited

- On Thursday, June 20, 2013, Members and staff toured the FedEx facilities with senior officers from the FedEx Corporation. The tour included the flight simulators FedEx uses to train their pilots, a discussion of the 33-foot double trailer configuration, the box matrix sorting facility, and the small package sorting facility.
- On Friday, June 21, 2013, Members and staff received a briefing on inland waterways issues and the Port of Memphis from the Executive Director of the port, a senior United States Army Corps of Engineers official, and a plant manager for Cargill; toured the port facilities; and

met with freight stakeholders at the Mid-South Community College in West Memphis, Arkansas.

APPENDIX K. SUMMARY OF SITE VISIT – NEW YORK CITY REGION

Overview

In order to gain a better understanding of freight movement in the region and to hear from local stakeholders, members and staff of the Panel on 21st Century Freight Transportation traveled to the New York City region from Thursday, July 25 to Saturday, July 27, 2013.

Sites Visited

- On Thursday, July 25, 2013, Members and staff departed Washington Union Station aboard a Norfolk Southern train. Senior Norfolk Southern officers briefed Members and staff on key freight facilities in the Northeast Corridor during the trip. Members and staff met officials from the Port Authority of New York and New Jersey upon arrival at the Oak Island Rail Yard. Members and staff then traveled to the Maher Terminal at the Port of Newark for a briefing on the Bayonne Bridge project and Port Authority operations.
- On Friday, July 26, 2013, Members and staff departed for the Greenville Yard in Jersey City, NJ with senior Port Authority officials for a briefing regarding New York/New Jersey cross harbor freight movement. Members and staff observed the loading of the New York New Jersey Railroad rail car ferry at the Greenville Yard intermodal facility. Next, Members and staff boarded a United States Army Corps of Engineers vessel for a boat tour shadowing the rail car ferry across New York Harbor. Members and staff arrived in Brooklyn and observed the unloading of the rail car ferry and the connection with the New York and Atlantic Railway, a local short-line railroad. Members of the Freight Panel conducted a field hearing at the Alexander Hamilton Custom House in Manhattan on "How Freight Transportation Challenges in Urban Areas Impact the Nation."

- On Saturday, July 27, 2013, staff toured the World Trade Center construction site with a Port Authority construction engineer. The tour included visits to the construction site for the Port Authority Trans-Hudson (PATH) transit terminal at the World Transit Center.

APPENDIX L. SUMMARY OF SITE VISIT – NORFOLK, VIRGINIA

Overview

In order to gain a better understanding of the operations at the Port of Virginia and at the Norfolk Southern Coal Pier 6, staff for the Panel on 21st Century Freight Transportation traveled to Norfolk, Virginia on Thursday, August 22 and Friday, August 23, 2013.

Sites Visited

- On Thursday, August 22, 2013, staff toured the Norfolk International Terminal and received a briefing on port operations. The chief of the port police force was also present to discuss port security issues. Next, staff departed for the APM terminal, a state of the art, privately-owned and constructed terminal that is operated by the Port of Virginia under a lease agreement with Maersk. Staff visited and were briefed at both a traditional container loading facility and an automated container facility. Security and coordination of vessels with both rail and truck land-side transport were reviewed. At the completion of the container review, staff boarded the vessel CMA CGM Samson for a tour and discussion on ship container loading and transport, and a working lunch with vessel crew. Later, staff departed for the United States Coast Guard Base Portsmouth for a briefing on Coast Guard operations with the Captain of the region. Discussions focused on the management of the harbor, safety protocols and issues associated with coordinating vessel traffic in and out of the harbor facilities. Staff also toured the Craney Island facility, which is used by the Port of Virginia to store dredge material and is the future site of terminal expansion at the Port of Norfolk.

- On Friday, August 23, 2013, staff received a briefing on the Norfolk Southern Coal Pier 6 and were given a tour of operations at the pier.

APPENDIX M. SUMMARY OF ROUNDTABLE POLICY DISCUSSION – "COORDINATING FEDERAL EFFORTS TO IMPROVE FREIGHT TRANSPORTATION"

Overview

The Panel on 21st Century Freight Transportation met on Wednesday, May 15, 2013, at 10:00 a.m., in 2253 Rayburn House Office Building to participate in a roundtable discussion on federal efforts to improve freight transportation. The Panel heard from participants from the United States Department of Transportation (DOT) and the United States Army Corps of Engineers.

Points of Discussion

- DOT has the primary responsibility in the Administration to develop freight transportation policy; the United States Army Corps of Engineers (Corps) also plays a role in transportation infrastructure. Specific to freight transportation, the Corps carries out construction and maintenance of navigation channels and the inland waterways system which are critical pieces of the Nation's freight transportation system.
- These two departments work together through a Memorandum of Understanding, establishing a collaborative relationship to improve the Nation's transportation system and infrastructure.
- The Freight Policy Council, created by DOT in August 2012, has been working with states to develop state freight plans as required by Section 1118 of the Moving Ahead for Progress in the 21st Century Act. MAP-21 also requires the development of a National Freight Strategic Plan to assess the conditions and performance of the National Freight Network, identifying points of congestion, forecasting freight volumes, and identifying major trade gateways, among other objectives.

- The National Freight Network is required by Section 1115 of MAP-21 to be designated by October 1, 2013; DOT is currently in the process of meeting this requirement. This primary freight network will consist of 27,000 centerline miles of existing roadways, with the option of expanding this limitation by no more than 3,000 additional centerline miles. The purpose of this network is to identify the infrastructure facilities that are most important to the movement of freight on the Nation's highways.

Participants

The Honorable John Porcari, Deputy Secretary
United States Department of Transportation

The Honorable Jo-Ellen Darcy, Assistant Secretary (Civil Works)
United States Department of the Army

APPENDIX N. SUMMARY OF ROUNDTABLE POLICY DISCUSSION – "NAVIGATING THE COMPLEXITIES OF AMERICA'S LARGEST PORT FACILITIES"

Overview

The Panel on 21st Century Freight Transportation met on Wednesday, May 29, 2013, at 1:30 p.m., at the Port of Los Angeles Administration building, located at 425 South Palos Verdes Street, San Pedro, California to participate in a roundtable discussion on port facilities and freight transportation. The Panel heard from stakeholders in the Southern California freight transportation community.

Points of Discussion

- As one of the most important trade gateways in the country, the freight system in Southern California is multimodal, incorporating ports, international border crossings, interstate highways, railroads, air cargo facilities, refrigeration facilities, and distribution and warehouse clusters.

- There are many infrastructure, capacity, and efficiency challenges facing the Ports of Los Angeles and Long Beach to maintain their competitiveness in the global economy. As the eighth largest port facility in the world, taken together, both Ports are undergoing major capital improvements to fight these challenges and to strengthen the national freight system.
- The Ports of Los Angeles and Long Beach handle more than 40 percent of all containers entering the United States and contribute an import tax to the Harbor Maintenance Trust Fund. The Ports of LA and Long Beach receive back less money than they pay into the Harbor Maintenance Trust Fund.
- Improving the efficiency of moving cargo through the harbor complex requires coordination between the Department of Homeland Security and the United States Coast Guard to ensure safety in the transport of materials in and out of the harbor. Both ports are investing in expanding container facilities to accommodate post-Panamax sized vessels.
- Given the challenges affecting this region, the importance of sustainable, long-term funding for transportation infrastructure in delivering freight projects is the key to a successful economic future for the Nation's freight system.

Participants

Chris Lytle, Executive Director
Port of Long Beach

Michael Christensen, Deputy Executive Director
Port of Los Angeles

Jeff Burgin, Senior Vice President and Chief Operating Officer
Pasha Stevedoring & Terminals

Alan McCorkle, Senior Vice President
APM Terminals

Victor La Rosa, President and Chief Executive Officer
Total Transportation Services, Inc.
Michael Antonovich, Chairman
Metropolitan Transportation Authority
Michael Gasparo, Manager for Ship Assist
Crowley

Rav Familathe, International Vice President (Mainland)
International Longshore and Warehouse Union

APPENDIX O. SUMMARY OF ROUNDTABLE POLICY DISCUSSION – "EFFECTIVELY COORDINATING FREIGHT PLANNING ACTIVITIES"

Overview

The Panel on 21st Century Freight Transportation met on Wednesday, July 17, 2013, at 10:00 a.m., in 2253 Rayburn House Office Building to participate in a roundtable discussion on effectively coordinating freight planning activities. The Panel heard from planning officials at the federal, state, regional, and local levels.

Points of Discussion

- Planning is key to any functioning transportation system, and freight planning itself is complicated because it involves multiple jurisdictions and require significant coordination among several parties.
- State departments of transportation, metropolitan planning organizations (MPOs), and rural planning commissions work together to create a statewide transportation improvement plan with proposals for future consideration. The Moving Ahead for Progress in the 21st Century Act created a new apportionment for metropolitan planning, requiring states to make more funds available for MPOs.
- Since freight projects are usually complex and involve several different parties, planning for and advancing these projects requires

significant coordination. The Panel heard suggestions on how freight planning stakeholders can effectively coordinate efforts to ensure the timely and well planned delivery of freight transportation facilities and whether additional ways for these entities to cooperate on the planning of large freight projects can be identified.

- There are a number of challenges that may impede the effective coordination of the planning for large freight projects, especially since freight projects often cross state boundaries, implicating multiple state departments of transportation and MPOs.

Participants

The Honorable Polly Trottenberg, Undersecretary for Policy
United States Department of Transportation

Richard Biter, Assistant Secretary for Intermodal Systems Development
Florida Department of Transportation

Don Kopec, Deputy Executive Director for Programming and Operations
Chicago Metropolitan Agency for Planning

Amy Kessler, Director of Community Development and Regional Planning
North Central Pennsylvania Regional Planning and Development Commission

Andrew Lynn, Director of Planning and Regional Development
Port Authority of New York and New Jersey

APPENDIX P. ACRONYM LIST

3PL	Third-Party Logistics
AATF	Airport and Airway Trust Fund
AIP	Airport Improvement Program
CREATE	Chicago Region Environmental and Transportation Efficiency Program
DOT	United States Department of Transportation

EAS	Essential Air Services
FAA	Federal Aviation Administration
FERC	Federal Energy Regulatory Commission
FHWA	Federal Highway Administration
HMT	Harbor Maintenance Tax
HMTF	Harbor Maintenance Trust Fund
HTF	Highway Trust Fund
HVUT	Heavy Vehicle Use Tax
ISTEA	Intermodal Surface Transportation Efficiency Act
IWTF	Inland Waterway Trust Fund
JIT	Just-in-Time Delivery
MAP-21	Moving Ahead for Progress in the 21st Century Act
MPO	Metropolitan Planning Organization
NEPA	National Environmental Policy Act
NextGen	Next Generation Air Transportation System
O&M	Operation and Maintenance
PHMSA	Pipelines and Hazardous Materials Safety Administration
PNRS	Projects of National and Regional Significance
PPP	Public-Private Partnership
PTC	Positive Train Control
RTM	Revenue Ton Mile
SAFETEA-LU	Safe, Accountable, Flexible, Efficient Transportation Equity Act: A Legacy for Users
STIP	Statewide Transportation Improvement Plan
TEA-21	Transportation Equity Act for the 21st Century
TEU	Twenty-foot Equivalent Unit
TIFIA	Transportation Infrastructure Finance and Innovation Act
TIGER	Transportation Investment Generating Economic Recovery
TTI	Texas Transportation Institute
VMT	Vehicle Miles Traveled
WRDA	Water Resources Development Act

End Notes

[1] U.S. CONST. pmbl.
[2] U.S. CONST. art. I, § 8, cl. 7.

[3] U.S. DEP'T OF TRANSP., FED. HIGHWAY ADMIN. (fHwa), FREIGHT FACTS AND FIGURES REPORT 10 (2012); U.S. DEP'T OF tRANSP., rESEARCH AND iNNOVATIVE tECH. aDMIN. (rita), TRANSP. STATISTICS ANNUAL REPORT 1 (2012).

[4] *Freight Facts and figures Report, at 9.*

[5] *Freight Transportation in America: Options for Improving the Nation's Network Before the S. Comm. on Commerce, Science, and Transp.*, 111th Cong. 1 (2009) (statement of Rick Gabrielson, Senior Dir. of Int'l Transp., Target).

[6] Postal Service Appropriations Act of 1912, Pub. L. No. 336, 37 Stat. 539 (1912).

[7] Federal Aid Highway Act of 1944, Pub. L. No. 78-521, 58 Stat. 838 (1944).

[8] Federal-Aid Highway Act of 1956, Pub. L. No. 84-627, 70 Stat. 374 (1956).

[9] FHWA, FINANCING FEDERAL-AID HIGHWAYS (2007).

[10] Surface Transportation Assistance Act of 1982, Pub. L. No. 97-424, 96 Stat. 2097 (1982).

[11] FINANCING FEDERAL-AID HIGHWAYS.

[12] *Id.*

[13] Transportation Equity Act for the 21st Century, Pub. L. No. 105-178; Safe, Accountable, Flexible, Efficient Transportation Equity Act: A Legacy for Users, Pub. L. No. 109-59; Moving Ahead for Progress in the 21st Century Act, Pub. L. No. 112-141.

[14] *How the Financial Status of the Highway Trust Fund Impacts Surface Transportation Programs Before the H. Comm. on Transp. & Infrastructure Subcomm. on Highways & Transit*, 113th Cong. 1 (2013) (statement of Kim P. Cawley, Chief, Natural & Physical Resources Cost Estimates Unit, Congressional Budget Office).

[15] *Id.*

[16] Pub. L. No. 84-627, § 108(c).

[17] *Id.*

[18] Pub. L. No. 84-627, § 108(a).

[19] Intermodal Surface Transportation Efficiency Act of 1991, Pub. L. No. 102-240, 105 Stat. 1914 (1991).

[20] *Id.*

[21] FHWA & FED. TRANSIT ADMIN. (FTA), CONDITIONS AND PERFORMANCE REPORT TO CONGRESS (2010).

[22] Moving Ahead for Progress in the 21st Century Act, Pub. L. No. 112-141 § 1101(a) (1).

[23] CONDITIONS AND PERFORMANCE REPORT.

[24] *Id.*, at 7-17.

[25] *Id.*, at 7-27.

[26] FREIGHT FACTS AND FIGURES REPORT, at 10.

[27] *Id.*, at 11.

[28] *Id.*, at 20.

[29] *Id.*, at 42.

[30] CONDITIONS AND PERFORMANCE REPORT, at 2-8.

[31] DAVID SCHRANK ET AL., TEXAS TRANSPORTATION INSTITUTE URBAN MOBILITY REPORT 5 (2012), *available at* http://tti.tamu.edu/documents/mobility-report-2012-wappx.pdf.

[32] *Id.*, at 5.

[33] *Id.*

[34] *Id.*, at 8.

[35] *Id.*, at 5.

[36] INRIX, TRAFFIC SCORECARD ANNUAL REPORT (2012-13), *available at* http://scorecard.inrix.com/scorecard/summary.asp.

[37] *Id.*

[38] MOBILITY-21, FREIGHT MOVEMENT INFRASTRUCTURE KEEPS OUR ECONOMY COMPETITIVE, *available at* http://mobility21.com/wp-content/uploads/2013/02/13dc_goodsmovement trifold_FINAL_lr.pdf.

[39] PORT OF LOS ANGELES, PORT OF LONG BEACH & ALAMEDA CORRIDOR TRANSPORTATION AUTHORITY, SAN PEDRO BAY PORTS NATIONAL ECONOMIC TRADE IMPACT REPORT (2013), *distributed to Panel in May, 2013.*

[40] TRADE PARTNERSHIP WORLDWIDE, IMPORTS WORK FOR AMERICA (2013), *available at* http://www.uschamber.com/sites/default/files/reports/ImportsWork_FIN.pdf.

[41] UNITED SOYBEAN BOARD ET AL., FARM TO MARKET: a SOYBEAN'S JOURNEY FROM FELD TO CONSUMER (2012), *available at* http://www.soytransportation.org/FarmToMarket/FarmToMarketStudy082012Study.pdf.

[42] FREIGHT FACTS AND FIGURES REPORT, at 10; TRANSPORTATION STATISTICS ANNUAL REPORT, at 1.

[43] MINNESOTA DEPARTMENT OF TRANSPORTATION, ECONOMIC IMPACTS OF I-35W BRIDGE COLLAPSE, *available at* http://www.dot.state. mn.us/i35wbridge/rebuild/municipal-consent/economic-impact.pdf.

[44] BRIAN SOLOMON, AMERICAN STEAM LOCOMOTIVE 11 (1998).

[45] Pacific Railroad Act of 1862, 12 Stat. 489.

[46] ASSOCIATION OF AMERICAN RAILROADS (AAR), OVERVIEW OF AMERICA'S FREIGHT RAILROADS 2 (2013), *available at* https://www. aar.org/keyissues/Documents/Background-Papers/Overview-US-Freight-RRs.pdf.

[47] FEDERAL RAILROAD ADMINISTRATION, FREIGHT RAIL TODAY; AMERICAN SHORT LINE AND REGIONAL RAILROAD ASSOCIATION (ASLRRA), STRENGTHENING AMERICA'S ECONOMY, available at http://www.aslrra.org/images/ASLRRA_FS_PZ_Strengthening.pdf.

[48] 49 C.F.R. § 1201 (2012).

[49] *Id.*

[50] AAR, CLASS I RAILROAD STATISTICS 1 (2013), *available at* https://www.aar.org/STATISTICSANDPUBLICATIONS/Documents/AAR-Stats-2013-04-17.pdf.

[51] CORRIDORS OF COMMERCE, ECONOMIC DEVELOPMENT, *available at* http://www. tradecorridors.com/benefits-of-rail/economic-development.

[52] *Id.*

[53] *Freight and Passenger Rail in America's Transportation System Before the H. Comm. On Transp. & Infrastructure Subcomm. on Railroads, Pipelines & Hazardous Materials*, 113th Cong. 1 (2013) (statement of Edward R. Hamberger, Pres. & CEO, Ass'n of Am. Railroads).

[54] Staggers Rail Act of 1980, Pub. L. No. 96-448, 94 Stat. 1895 (1980); Interstate Commerce Commission Termination Act of 1995, Pub. L. No. 104-88, 109 Stat. 803 (1995).

[55] Jean-Paul Rodrigue, et al., *The Geography of Transport Systems*, Hofstra University, Department of Global Studies & Geography (2013), *available at* http://people.hofstra.edu/geotrans; *Brian Slack, Rail Deregulation in the United States*, Hofstra University, Department of Global Studies & Geography (2013), *available at* http://people.hofstra.edu/geotrans/eng/ch9en/appl9en/ch9a1en.html.

[56] ANNE CANBY, AMERICA'S RAIL SYSTEM, available atbriefing-rail-system-overview-final-2-22-13.pdf.

[57] AAR, CLASS I RAILROAD STATISTICS, at 1; ASLRRA, STRENGTHENING AMERICA'S ECONOMY, at 1.

[58] AAR, COLLECTIVE BARGAINING IN THE RAIL INDUSTRY 1 (2013), available at https://www.aar.org/keyissues/Documents/Background-Papers/Collective-Bargaining.pdf.

[59] Railway Labor Act, 44 Stat. 577 (1926).

[60] COLLECTIVE BARGAINING IN THE RAIL INDUSTRY, at 1.

[61] *Id.*

[62] The 13 major rail unions are: the American Train Dispatchers Association, the Brotherhood of Railroad Signalmen, the International Association of Machinists and Aerospace Workers, the International Brotherhood of Boilermakers, Blacksmiths, Forgers and Helpers, the International Brotherhood of Electrical Workers, the National Conference of Firemen and Oilers SEIU, the Sheet Metal Workers International Association, the Transportation

Communications International Union, the Transport Workers Union of America, the United Transportation Union, UNITE-HERE, the Brotherhood of Locomotive Engineers and Trainmen Division of the International Brotherhood of Teamsters, and the Brotherhood of Maintenance of Way Employees Division of the International Brotherhood of Teamsters.

[63] *Anthony J. Mayo & Nitin Nohria, The Truck Driver Who Reinvented Shipping* (2005) (excerpted from *In Their Time: The Greatest Business Leaders of the Twentieth Century*), *available at* http://hbswk.hbs.edu/item/5026.html.

[64] FREIGHT FACTS AND FIGURES REPORT, at 15.

[65] WORLD SHIPPING COUNCIL, TRADE STATISTICS, *available at* http://www.worldshipping.org/about-the-industry/global-trade/trade-statistics.

[66] Am. Ass'n of Port Authorities (AAPA), U.S. Public Port Facts (2008).

[67] AM. ASS'N OF STATE HIGHWAY AND TRANSP. OFFICIALS (aaSHto), WATERBORNE FREIGHT TRANSPORTATION 2-2 (2013), *available at* http://water.transportation.org/SiteCollection Documents/WFT-1.pdf.

[68] Water Resources Development Act of 1986, Pub. L. No. 99–662, 100 Stat. 4082 (1986).

[69] AAPA, GOVERNMENT RELATIONS PRIORITIES: WATER RESOURCES 1 (2013), *available at* http://www.aapa-ports.org/files/Water%20Resources%202013_1363709492636_1.pdf.

[70] *Id.*

[71] John Frittelli, *Harbor Maintenance Trust Fund Expenditures*, CONGRESSIONAL RESEARCH SERVICE, Report No. R41042, January 10, 2011, at 5.

[72] *Id.*

[73] *Id.*

[74] *Id.*, at 7.

[75] *Id.*

[76] STAFF OF JOINT COMM. ON TAXATION, 112TH CONG., OVERVIEW OF SELECTED TAX PROVISIONS RELATING TO THE fINANCING OF INFRASTRUCTURE 18 (JCX-29-11).

[77] DEP'T OF THE TREASURY, HARBOR MAINTENANCE TRUST FUND, Rep. No. 96X8863.

[78] *Harbor Maintenance Trust Fund Expenditures*, at 8-9.

[79] AASHTO, WATERBORNE FREIGHT TRANSPORTATION, at 2-10.

[80] SHIP AND BUNKER, NAVIGATING THE ARCTIC'S ICY WATERS (2013), *available at* http://shipandbunker.com/news/world/471456-fathom-spotlight-navigating-the-arctics-icy-waters.

[81] Jean-Paul Rodrigue, et al., *The Geography of Transport Systems: Polar Shipping Routes*, Hofstra University, Department of Global Studies & Geography (2013), *available at* http://people.hofstra.edu/geotrans/eng/ch1en/conc1en/polarroutes.html.

[82] U.S. ARMY CORPS OF ENGINEERS, INLAND WATERWAY NAVIGATION: VALUE TO THE NATION, available at http://www.sas.usace.army.mil/Portals/61/docs/lakes/thurmond/navigate.pdf.

[83] AASHTO, WATERBORNE FREIGHT TRANSPORTATION, at 3-1.

[84] *Id.*

[85] *Budget Hearing – United States Army Corps of Engineers Before the H. Comm. on Appropriations Subcomm. on Energy and Water Dev., & Related Agencies*, 113th Cong. 1 (2013) (statement of Am. Society of Civil Engineers).

[86] NAT'L WATERWAYS FOUND., WATERWAYS: WORKING FOR AMERICA 2 (2012), *available at* http://www.nationalwaterwaysfoundation.org/study/NWF_117900_2011WorkingForAmericaBrochure_FINAL_forWeb.pdf.

[87] *Id.*

[88] INLAND WATERWAY NAVIGATION: VALUE TO THE NATION.

[89] THE AMERICAN WATERWAYS OPERATORS, JOBS & ECONOMY: INDUSTRY FACTS (2013), *available at* http://www.americanwaterways.com/initiatives/jobs-economy/industry-facts.

[90] TENNESSEE VALLEY AUTHORITY, ECONOMIC SIGNIFICANCE, *available at* http://www.tva.gov/river/navigation/economic.htm.

[91] Water Resources Development Act of 1986, Pub. L. No. 99–662, 100 Stat. 4082 (1986).

[92] Charles V. Stern, *Inland Waterways: Recent Proposals and Issues for Congress*, CONGRESSIONAL RESEARCH SERVICE, Report No. R41430, May 3, 2013, at 9.
[93] Water Resources Development Act of 1986, Pub. L. No. 99–662, 100 Stat. 4082 (1986).
[94] *Inland Waterways: Recent Proposals and Issues for Congress*, at 10.
[95] Airport and Airway Development and Revenue Act of 1970, Pub. L. No. 91-258 (1970).
[96] FEDERAL AVIATION ADMINISTRATION, AIRPORT AND AIRWAY TRUST FUND FACT SHEET 2 (2013).
[97] Airport and Airway Improvement Act of 1982, Pub. L. No. 97-248 (1982).
[98] AIRPORT AND AIRWAY TRUST FUND FACT SHEET, at 5.
[99] *Id.*, at 6.
[100] *How Logistics Facilitate an Efficient Freight Transportation System Before the H. Comm. on Transp. & Infrastructure Panel on 21st Century Freight Transp.*, 113th Cong. 1 (2013) (statement of Richard H. Fisher, Pres., Falcon Global Edge).
[101] FEDERAL AVIATION ADMINISTRATION (FAA), AEROSPACE FORECAST FOR FISCAL YEARS 2013-2033 15 (2013), *available at* http://www.faa.gov/about/office_org/headquarters_offices/apl/aviation_forecasts/aerospace_forecasts/2013-2033/media/2013_Forecast.pdf.
[102] A revenue ton mile (RTM) is the movement of one ton of freight one mile for revenue.
[103] AEROSPACE FORECAST FOR FISCAL YEARS 2013-2033, at 24.
[104] LOS ANGELES WORLD AIRPORTS, AIR FREIGHT AT LOS ANGELES WORLD AIRPORTS (2013), *distributed to Panel in May, 2013.*
[105] Joseph Bonney, *3PL Learning Curve*, JOURNAL OF COMMERCE, Sept. 2011, at 4A.
[106] DEP'T OF COMMERCE, THE LOGISTICS & TRANSP. INDUS. IN THE U.S., *available at* http://selectusa.commerce.gov/industry-snap>shots/logistics-and-transportation-industry-united-states.
[107] RICHARD ARMSTRONG, U.S. 3pl MARKET GROWS 7%: OUTPACES ECONOMY, AVAILABLE AT HTTP://WWW.3PLOGISTICS.COM
[108] *Thomas Meadows & Company, Understanding the Freight Business* (London: The Company, 1978).
[109] *Id.*
[110] *Id.*
[111] TRANSP. INTERMEDIARIES ASS'N (tia), ABOUT THE INDUS., *available at* http://www.tianet.org/AM/Template.cfm?Section=Edu>*cation.*
[112] *Id.*
[113] COUNCIL OF SUPPLY CHAIN MANAGEMENT PROFESSIONALS, SUPPLY CHAIN MANAGEMENT, *available at* http://cscmp.org/about-us/supply-chain-management-definitions.
[114] *How Logistics Facilitate an Efficient Freight Transportation System Before the H. Comm. on Transp. & Infrastructure Panel on 21st Century Freight Transp.*, 113th Cong. 1 (2013) (statement of Mark V. DeFabis, Pres. & CEO, Integrated Distribution Services, Inc.).
[115] JOHN G. LARKIN, ET AL., TRANSP. & LOGISTICS: INDUS. UPDATE (2012), *available at* http://www.tianet.org/staticcontent/stat>*icpages/06-07*-2012_Robert_Voltmann_Stifel_Nicolaus_Call.pdf.
[116] DNV GL, HAZARDOUS LIQUID AND NATURAL GAS TRANSMISSION PIPELINES (2013), *distributed to Panel in October, 2013.*
[117] *Id.*, at 13.
[118] *Id.*, at 12.
[119] *Id.*
[120] *Id.*, at 6.
[121] FREIGHT FACTS AND FIGURES REPORT, at 9.
[122] HAZARDOUS LIQUID AND NATURAL GAS TRANSMISSION PIPELINES, at 5.

In: U.S. Freight Transportation
Editor: Alaina Hutson
ISBN: 978-1-63321-235-0

Chapter 2

STATEMENT OF DEREK J. LEATHERS, PRESIDENT AND CEO, WERNER ENTERPRISES, INC. HEARING ON ''OVERVIEW OF THE UNITED STATES' FREIGHT TRANSPORTATION SYSTEM''*

INTRODUCTION

Chairman Duncan, Ranking Member Nadler, and members of the panel, thank you for giving me the opportunity to testify at the first hearing of this special panel on behalf of Werner Enterprises, Inc. Werner is a member the American Trucking Associations, Inc. (ATA), and the views expressed in my testimony are consistent with ATA's positions. I would also like to commend Chairman Shuster and Ranking Member Rahall for creating this panel in recognition of the importance that freight plays in our nation's economy. I look forward to working with this panel and the full committee to craft a surface transportation reauthorization bill that promotes the safe, clean, and efficient movement of goods.

I am President and COO of Werner Enterprises, Inc., a premier transportation and logistics company, founded in 1956, with coverage throughout North America, Asia, Europe, South America, Africa and Australia. Werner maintains its global headquarters in Omaha, Nebraska.

* This is an edited, reformatted and augmented version of statement presented April 24, 2013 before the Panel on 21st Century Freight Transportation.

Werner is one of the five largest truckload carriers in the United States, with a diversified portfolio of transportation services that includes dedicated; medium-to-long-haul, regional and local van; expedited; temperature-controlled; and flatbed services. Werner's Value Added Services portfolio includes freight management, truck brokerage, intermodal, and international services. International services are provided through Werner's domestic and global subsidiary companies and include ocean, air and ground transportation; freight forwarding; and customs brokerage. We have more than 7,250 tractors, nearly 25,000 trailers and over 13,000 employees and independent contractors.

Mr. Chairman, a safe, efficient system of highways connecting America's cities, towns and rural areas is essential to our country's economic well-being, military security, and overall quality of life. Your predecessors recognized the necessity of good road transportation by creating the Interstate Highway System, which has served our country well, and today allows even the smallest entrepreneur to access markets throughout the country and around the world.

Every day, thousands of trailers and containers, carrying everything from grain to machine parts, flow through our ports, across our borders, and on our highway, rail, air and waterway systems, as part of a global multimodal transportation logistics system. It is a complex array of moving parts that provides millions of jobs to Americans, broadens the choices of products on store shelves, and creates new and expanding markets for U.S. businesses. Highways are the key to this system. Trucks move 68% of our Nation's freight tonnage and draw 81% of freight revenue.[1] In addition, trucks move $8.3 trillion worth of freight each year, nearly 60% of the U.S. economy,[2] and the trucking industry is expected to move an even greater share of freight in the future.[3] Trucks are also crucial to freight moved by rail, air, and water. The highway system connects all of these modes to manufacturing and assembly plants, warehouses, retail outlets, and homes. An efficient highway system is the key to a fluid global supply chain, which in turn is a fundamental element of a growing and prosperous economy. It should also be noted that despite the emphasis on promoting the use of intermodal transportation for moving our Nation's freight, *93% of freight moves by a single mode.*[4]

The share of additional freight that could benefit from intermodal service is extremely small, and the vast majority of freight will continue to be carried by trucks on the highway system.

THE TRUCKING INDUSTRY CONTINUES TO GET SAFER

Safety is the trucking industry's highest priority. Industry-supported federal regulations, combined with better training, advanced safety technology and a greater focus by carriers on creating a better safety culture within their companies, have produced tremendously positive results. Over the past decade, the number of truck-related fatalities has decreased by 24% and the number of injuries has been reduced by 39%, despite steady growth in the overall number of trucks and miles on the road.

Unfortunately, new hours of service regulations that are scheduled to take effect in July will reduce industry productivity by 2-3%, without offsetting safety benefits. *As* such, it will take more drivers and trucks to move the same amount of freight. Furthermore, the rules will have the unintended safety consequence of putting more trucks on the road during morning peak travel periods. And, the new, unjustified provisions will make compliance more complex. In addition, a growing lack of truck parking along major truck corridors- which will be exacerbated by the new HOS rules- is making it increasingly difficult for drivers to get their needed rest and comply with federal regulations.

Mr. Chairman, while we are pleased with our progress, we believe that the industry's best days are before us. The development and adoption of new on-board technology, such as stability control and forward collision mitigation systems, will significantly reduce truck- involved crashes. We urge Congress to support these advances.

THE TRUCKING INDUSTRY IS CLEANER THAN EVER

Each new truck purchased today produces 90% less particulate matter (PM) and nitrogen oxides (NOx) emissions than a decade ago. To put this improvement into perspective, the emissions from 60 new trucks purchased today roughly equals the emissions produced by a single new truck purchased in the mid 1980s, when truck emission standards were first established. Trucking was the first freight mode to widely use advanced diesel engine emission control systems. In 2002, the trucking industry began buying new trucks which incorporated exhaust gas recirculation

(EGR), which combined with other emission control technologies to reduce tailpipe emissions of NOx by half. In addition, as of 2010, all on-highway diesel fuel sold in the United States contains near- zero levels of sulfur (<15 parts/million).

ATA launched a proactive industry-wide sustainability plan in 2008 to reduce greenhouse gas emissions by nearly one billion tons and fuel consumption by over 86 billion gallons over a ten-year period. ATA helped to develop and is a Charter Partner of the EPA SmartWay Transp01t Partnership's voluntary greenhouse gas reduction program, which includes close to 3,000 trucking fleets. Launched in 2004, fleets have saved 55 million barrels of oil, the equivalent of taking over 3 million cars off the road for an entire year. SmartWay's clean air achievements- 24 million metric tons of carbon dioxide, 478,000 metric tons of nitrogen oxides, and 24,000 metric tons of particulate matter reduced so far – help to protect public health.

Finally, greenhouse gas and fuel economy standards will take effect for new trucks beginning with model year 2014 equipment. It has been estimated that this new rule will reduce $C0_2$ emissions by about 298 million tons and save approximately 530 million barrels of oil over the life of model year 2014 to 2018 vehicles.

Condition and Performance of the Highway System

Mr. Chairman, the highway system is the lifeblood of the trucking industry and the key to moving America's freight. Unfortunately, the system no longer meets our transportation needs. A new report from the Texas Transportation Institute at Texas A&M University confirms what many of us already know: that in many American cities traffic gridlock is not only frustrating and time-consuming, it is also extremely expensive. TTI's *2012 Urban Mobility Report* found that congestion in 498 U.S. cities cost the economy $121 billion in 2011, up from an inflation-adjusted $24 billion in 1982. The report determined that $27 billion of the 2011 costs were borne by the trucking industry, and passed on to customers and, ultimately, consumers.

However, our highway woes are not just limited to congestion. According to the American Society of Civil Engineers (ASCE), 31% of travel occurs on deficient pavement, resulting in higher freight costs due to greater vehicle operating expenditures and more potential for damaged goods [5] Furthermore, the Federal Highway Administration reports [6] that more than 100,000 bridges are structurally deficient or functionally obsolete, which means that these structures will need either major improvements or will have to be replaced, at enormous cost. In addition, 3,600 bridges are in such poor condition that they have been closed, and 61,000 have been load-posted, forcing trucks to re-route, adding miles and cost to deliveries.

What is being done to address these problems? Unfortunately, very little. ASCE reports that while the U.S. is currently investing $70 billion in our highways annually, an investment of $133 billion is necessary *just to prevent the situation from getting worse*. By 2020 the investment shortfall is projected to reach $756 billion and an unimaginable $3.25 *trillion* by 2040.[7]

The most recent Conditions and Performance Report by the Federal Highway Administration estimates that we need to invest $101 billion annually at all levels of government just to maintain today's substandard conditions and performance on our roads. To improve our road system, the C&P Report estimates that we would need to invest $170 billion annually.

The Interstate System, the larger National Highway System, and the soon to be designated "National Freight Network" must be our top priority. The NHS contains only 5% of the Nation's total route mileage but carries 55% of all vehicle miles travelled and 93% of truck VMT.

The federal Highway Trust Fund, which since 1956 has provided the bulk of funding for the Interstate Highway System and other major highways plied by IS-wheelers is, for all intents and purposes, bankrupt. The Fund, which normally relies almost exclusively on revenue from federal fuel taxes and truck fees, is being kept afloat by an annual infusion of nearly $10 billion in General Fund subsidies. As highway construction costs continue to escalate and vehicle fuel efficiency improves, that dependency will grow. In an era of massive federal budget deficits, the future of the federal-aid highway program is in serious jeopardy. Despite reports to the contrary, the fuel tax is still a viable source of revenue, and can continue to be the primary source of funding for highways for many years. However, the rate of taxation must be adjusted to account for inflation and fuel efficiency improvements. ATA supports an increase in the fuel tax rate, indexing of the tax rate, or a combination of the two. This is the most efficient and least harmful way to prevent a catastrophic collapse of the federal-aid highway program.

CREATE A NEW HIGHWAY FREIGHT PROGRAM

While more resources than are currently available will be necessary to fund the transportation improvements needed to get our country out of traffic gridlock, and to make driving less hazardous, we can no longer afford to spend federal resources on projects that do not meet our most important national needs. When the federal highway program was created, it had a clearly defined mission: to finance construction of the Interstate Highway System. When that mission was complete, highway user revenues were still flowing into the Highway Trust Fund, but Congress did not identify a new federal role. As a result, the federal-aid highway program has evolved into a block grant program for states, without a clear purpose.

MAP-21 took several steps toward remedying this situation, and the authors deserve credit for inserting language requiring recipients of federal aid to meet performance standards, including those related to freight transportation, and for ordering an identification of those highways essential to goods delivery. While MAP-21 did provide a greater federal share for certain freight projects, tight transportation budgets have greatly curtailed construction of new capacity, and it is unlikely that the bottlenecks identified under MAP-21 provisions will be funded with a greater priority than they were prior to the bill's passage. Therefore, ATA strongly recommends that Congress set aside money specifically for funding projects to eliminate bottlenecks identified under Section 1115 ofMAP-21. The highest priority should be given to bottlenecks on the Primary Freight Network. A study for FHWA [8] identified the highway bottlenecks that cause the greatest amount of delay for trucks. Based on the agency's estimates, ATA calculates that these bottlenecks cost the trucking industry approximately $19 billion per year in lost fuel, wages, and equipment utilization. The study estimated that highway bottlenecks account for 40% of congestion.

ATA also recommends dedicating a greater share of the federal-aid highway program to the newly expanded National Highway System, which carries 55% of all traffic and 97% of truck freight. Additionally, the NHS carries 98% of the value of truck trade with Canada and Mexico.[9]

SOURCES OF FUNDING

Trucking companies are willing to support an increase in the fuel tax if the revenues are dedicated to projects and programs that will benefit goods movement on the nation's highways. While we understand that a fuel tax increase is difficult for some Members to support, the fact remains that no other source of funding has been identified that –

- will produce the level of revenues needed to meet current and future highway infrastructure needs;
- is easy and inexpensive to pay and collect;
- has a low evasion rate;
- is tied to highway use; and
- does not create impediments to interstate commerce.

Private financing of highway infrastructure can play only a very limited role in addressing future transportation needs, and certain practices may generate unintended consequences whose costs will vastly exceed their short-term economic benefits. In particular, ATA is very concerned about attempts by some states to carve up the most important segments of the Interstate System for long-term lease to the highest bidder. Leasing existing Interstate highways to private interests is inconsistent with the efficient and cost effective movement of freight, is not in the public's best interest, and represents a vision for the Nation's transportation system that is short-sighted and ill-conceived. And to be blunt, privatization is the easy way out for politicians who want to avoid the tough decisions about raising user fees. We therefore oppose these schemes.

We are also concerned about the emphasis on TIFIA and other financing instruments. While they can be helpful under certain circumstances, they are not a substitute for "real" money. In fact, these types of mechanisms simply shift more of the burden for funding transportation from the federal to state and local levels since most of the financing costs must come from a non-federal source. It is important to keep in mind that projects which receive assistance under these types of programs will still require a "real" money funding source to pay back the principal, interest, and associated fees.

ATA is strongly opposed to tolls on existing Interstate highway capacity. While federal law generally prohibits this practice, Congress has, over the years, created a number of exceptions. Imposing tolls on existing lanes of the Interstate System would have a devastating effect on the trucking industry. The industry is highly competitive and tolls usually cannot be passed along to shippers. Furthermore, tolls cause diversion of traffic to alternative routes, which are usually less safe and were not built to handle the additional traffic. We urge Congress to eliminate the existing pilot programs which provide tolling authority for existing Interstate Highways and to refrain from authorizing additional tolling flexibility.

Finally, ATA has serious concerns about mileage-based user fees. While we recognize that in the future a replacement for the fuel tax as the primary source of revenue for highway funding will be necessary due to changes in vehicle technology, that future is likely two decades away at least. It is important to understand that passenger vehicle fleet conversion will precede commercial vehicles' transition from internal combustion engines by many years. Therefore, it would be illogical to require trucks to transition to a mileage-based fee before passenger vehicles.

Currently available options for implementing vehicle miles traveled fees are limited, and these options have extremely high collection costs, and will experience a very high level of evasion. A mileage-based fee would also be inefficient and very difficult to administer. Collection costs for the federal fuel tax are less than 1%. [10] Collection costs for Germany's truck VMT tax system, currently the most sophisticated VMT tax in the world, are approximately 23% of revenue. [11] Since the fee is imposed almost exclusively on the Autobahn, which has the greatest volume of traffic, and Germany's user fee rates far exceed levels that would be acceptable to U.S. drivers, this should be considered a conservative figure.

While it can be argued that technological advances and economies of scale will eventually bring costs down, the cost of administering the system will never come close to the cost of collecting the fuel tax. The fuel tax is collected from a few hundred taxpayers, while the VMT fee would have to be collected from tens of millions of individual taxpayers for each vehicle. In 2011, there were nearly 245 million registered vehicles in the U.S. Therefore, a bureaucracy would have to be established to deal with the same number of individual accounts. Compare this with the IRS, which processes less than 180 million tax returns each year. The physical and bureaucratic infrastructure necessary to effectively collect a VMT fee would have to be massive and the cost to both government and taxpayer would be enormous. Furthermore, because a VMT fee would have to rely on technology for monitoring and collection, significant enforcement challenges resulting from system tampering and equipment malfunction should be expected.[12]

The challenges facing fuel tax revenue over the next 20 years can be addressed by indexing the rate. Substituting an untested, highly inefficient revenue collection mechanism for an efficient revenue mechanism that is already in place would be illogical and irresponsible, and would receive significant resistance from the trucking industry and other highway users.

IMPROVE THE MOVEMENT OF INTERMODAL FREIGHT

While the vast majority of truck freight does not move as part of an intermodal delivery, intermodal freight is an important and growing part of the supply chain. It is also where significant bottlenecks occur.

ATA, along with our partners representing other modes, has long advocated for dedicated funding of last-mile intermodal connectors: those parts of the highway system that link ports, rail intermodal terminals and airports with the National Highway System. Many of these links have been described as "orphan roads" because while they are critical segments of the freight transportation system, they are often overlooked by the state or local governments responsible for them because many of their benefits accrue far beyond their borders.

Another barrier to the efficient movement of intermodal freight has to do with the condition and safety of chassis. Legislation introduced in this committee and enacted by Congress in 2005 established a statutory framework requiring intermodal chassis providers to ensure that their equipment (which is integral to the movement of millions of international freight containers transported in the intermodal sector each year) was in a safe "roadable" condition before it is used for transport. ATA's Intermodal Motor Carriers Conference (IMCC) was actively engaged in the Roadability legislative and regulatory negotiations, and the consensus statutory language that developed was embodied in section 4118 of the Safe, Accountable, Flexible, Efficient Transportation Equity Act: A Legacy for Users (SAFETEA-LU).

Unfortunately, implementation of the law has been slow, and overall compliance with the program's key legal mandates has not yet reached a level where the chassis that are moving on the highway system can be considered to be systematically maintained and repaired, and are in a roadable condition, as the law requires. The lack of roadable equipment slows down the movement of intermodal freight when equipment is taken out of service or drivers are forced to select new equipment when they fail a pre-trip inspection.

Moreover, intermodal drivers are now being charged during roadside inspections with equipment violations on the chassis that we believe should instead be assigned to the equipment provider, who is now supposed to be the responsible party. As a result of these regulatory enforcement practices, intermodal motor carrier/driver CSA scores are negatively and unfairly inflated by chassis deficiencies. With rising scores, we are beginning to see drivers leave the intermodal transport side of the business in order to avoid having their scores elevated by chassis deficiencies. This is exacerbating the intermodal driver shortage problem.

This failure to achieve the law's mandates is in large part due to FMCSA's decision to not require the driver's pre-trip chassis inspection to be documented and to not aggressively audit equipment provider operations to ensure that systematic maintenance and repair programs are in place. The only way to generate data on whether an equipment providing facility has an effective systematic maintenance and repair system, as required by law, is to document the driver pre-trip inspection, which is done when the provider first makes the chassis available for use. Since that data is not now being collected, we believe the agency does not have the requisite equipment provider system performance records needed to perform the required Roadability audits to actually measure and evaluate program performance. This lack of measurable progress has gone on for far too long. We urge you to review the chassis Roadability program, and work with FMCSA to ensure that the statutory changes that Congress put in place in 2005 are being implemented effectively.

AUTHORIZE THE USE OF MORE PRODUCTIVE TRUCKS

In addition to well-maintained, less congested highways and bridges, the trucking industry needs to improve its equipment utilization if it is to meet current and future demands. The United States has the most restrictive truck weight regulations of any developed country. At the same time, America's freight transportation demands are greater than that of any other nation, and we have the world's most well-developed highway system. Restrictive federal regulations governing the length and weight of trucks prevent the industry from operating its cleanest, safest, most efficient equipment.

Research demonstrates that more productive trucks can be as safe as or safer than existing configurations.[13] Furthermore, because fewer truck trips will be needed to haul a set amount of freight, crash exposure – and therefore the number of crashes – will be reduced.

More productive vehicles would also produce important environmental benefits by reducing vehicle miles traveled, fuel consumption, and greenhouse gas emissions. Use of these vehicles could result in a fuel usage reduction of up to 39%, with similar reductions in criteria and greenhouse gas emissions [14]

In addition, adding more weight can lower pavement costs·[15] Bridge costs can be minimized through effective bridge management, such as load posting bridges that are not designed for the additional weight, strengthening bridges where necessary, or replacing structures where it makes economic sense.[16]

Furthermore, Mr. Chairman, independent research predicts a net positive economic return from increased trucking productivity. A U.S. Department of Transpoltation study found that shipper costs could come down by as much as 11%.[17] A study by Oak Ridge National Labs concluded that the use of certain vehicles could reduce a shipper's logistics costs by between 13% and 32%[18] These savings are ultimately passed on to the consumer in the form of lower shelf prices. Furthermore, the U.S. has the lowest national weight limits of any developed country.[19] This puts American businesses at a disadvantage, and makes it more difficult for them to compete with companies in other nations. In order to take advantage of the benefits that productivity increases can deliver, Congress must reform its laws to give states greater flexibility to change their size and weight regulations, and should also modernize vehicle length standards.

We understand that Members may be reluctant to support changes to size and weight law until the MAP-21 study is released. However, there are hundreds of research reports already completed which support our proposals, and one more study will simply bolster the reforms we are proposing.

MODAL COMPETITION

Some have speculated that significant shifts in modal share would occur if size and weight limits increased or if the freight railroads were subsidized or given additional marketplace advantages through regulatory change, or if current regulations designed to protect their marketplace advantage were amended. This is a fallacy. Railroads and trucking companies serve very different markets, and rarely compete for freight. As the chart below shows, over the past two decades, through economic booms and busts, significant swings in energy costs, and the so-called "rail revolution," market shares have been very stable. Neither greater trucking productivity, nor incremental improvements in rail intermodal service, is likely to change this reality.

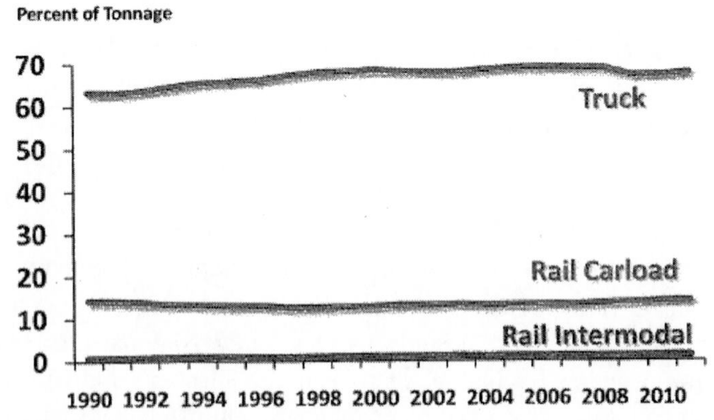

Source: U.S. Freight Transportation Forecast to 2023 (Publishers note: due to formatting limitations the original lines in the chart are not completely smooth and straight as shown above).

In fact, even if intermodal rail service volumes were to grow far more rapidly than projections, the impact on truck traffic would be virtually imperceptible, and would have, effectively, no impact on highway safety, emissions, or infrastructure maintenance and construction costs. In fact, even if rail intermodal volumes grew at twice the rate of projections over the next decade, the trucking industry's market share would dip by just 1%. A tripling of intermodal volumes would reduce truck market share by just 2%. Under both scenarios, truck market share would actually increase compared with today because trucks are expected to gain market share over this time period.

What we do know is that all modes are likely to .see increases in demand. By 2023 Class 8 trucks will move 76% more freight tonnage with 36% more vehicles. Meeting this challenge will be exceedingly difficult without a much greater, more strategic public investment in the highways that carry significant truck volumes, and a regulatory environment which allows for improved efficiencies. Obstructing trucking efficiency improvements by continuing to limit the industry's productivity with size and weight regulations that are unsubstantiated by science will not support an expanded economy or meet a growing population's needs.

We would also like to note that ATA members, including Werner Enterprises, are significant users of rail intermodal service, and trucking companies are among the railroads' largest customers. We find the railroads' opposition to improvements in trucking productivity to be counterintuitive given the already discussed market share data, the level of cooperation between the modes in the rail intermodal space, and the importance of trucking capacity to the current and future success of the intermodal market. Enhancing the productivity of trucks will benefit both rail intermodal and truck- only deliveries, and the ultimate result will be fewer emissions, less congestion and less crash risk to motorists as the number of trucks on the road comes down.

CONCLUSION

Mr. Chairman, thank you for the opportunity to offer our views on how, collectively, we can further improve truck and highway mobility. A strong federal highway program is necessary to achieve these goals, and significant additional resources must be made available to this purpose. We look forward to working with you to find the necessary resources to support the highest possible funding levels. However, even under the best scenario, funding will likely continue to fall well short of what is necessary to simply maintain the highway system, let alone tackle growing congestion. In the absence of new resources, the federal program should be reformed to ensure that revenues are invested in critical projects that serve the national interest. Furthermore, outdated size and weight regulations can and should be changed to improve the efficiency of our highway system.

End Notes

[1] Global Insight, U.S. Freight Transportation Forecast to.2023, 2012.
[2] U.S. Census Bureau, 2007 Commodity Flow Survey, Dec. 22, 2009.
[3] Global Insight, U.S. Freight Transportation Forecast to.2023, 2012.
[4] U.S. Census Bureau, 2007 Commodity Flow Survey, Dec. 22, 2009.
[5] American Society of Civil Engineers, 2013 Report Card for America's Infrastructure, 2013.
[6] Federal Highway Administration, National Bridge Inventory, Dec. 31,2012.
[7] American Society of Civil Engineers, 2013 Report Card for America's Infrastructure, 2013.
[8] Cambridge Systematics for the Federal Highway Administration, Estimated Cost of Freight Involved in Highway Bottlenecks, Nov. 12, 2008. ·
[9] U.S. Department of Transportation FY2014 Budget Highlights, April2013.
[10] Transportation Research Board NCHRP Report 689. Costs of Alternative Revenue-Generation Systems, 2011.
[11] Ibid.
[12] Texas Department of Transportation. Vehicle Mileage Fee Primer, p. 16. Dec. 2009.
[13] See for example: Campbell, K.L., et al., "Analysis of Accident Rates of Heavy-Duty Vehicles," University of Michigan Transportation Research Institute (UMTRl), Report No. UMTRl-88-17, Ann Arbor, MI. 1988.; Transportation Research Board, National Research Council, "Truck Weight Limits," Special Report 225, Washington, D.C., 1990; Cornell University School of Civil and Environmental Engineering, "Economic and Safety Consequences of Increased Truck Weights," Dec. 1987; Scientex, "Accident Rates For Longer Combination Vehicles," 1996; Woodrooffe and Assoc., "Longer Combination Vehicle Safety Performance in Alberta 1995 to 1998," March 2001; International Transport Forum, "Moving Freight with Better Trucks," 2010.
[14] American Transportation Research Institute, Energy and Emissions Impacts of Operating Higher Productivity Vehicles. March 2008.
[15] See for example: U.S. Department of Transportation. Comprehensive Truck Size and Weight Study. Washington D.C. August 2000.; Transportation Research Board. Regulation of Weights, Lengths, and Widths of Commercial Motor Vehicles. Special Report 267. Washington D.C. 2002.
[16] Transportation Research Board. Regulation of Weights, Lengths, and Widths Commercial Motor Vehicles. Special' Report 267. Washington D.C. 2002.
[17] U.S. Department of Transportation. Comprehensive Truck Size and Weight Study. Washington D.C. August 2000.
[18] Center for Transportation Analysis Energy Division, Oak Ridge National Laboratory, The Productivity Effects of Truck Size and Weight Policies, Nov. 1994.
[19] International Transport Forum, Moving Freight with Better Trucks, 2010.

In: U.S. Freight Transportation
Editor: Alaina Hutson
ISBN: 978-1-63321-235-0

Chapter 3

FEDERAL FREIGHT POLICY: IN BRIEF*

John Frittelli

FREIGHT SYSTEM COMPONENTS

The U.S. freight system is a complex network including four principal modes of transportation:

- The National Truck Network comprises 209,000 miles of highways that can accommodate large trucks, including the 47,000-mile Interstate Highway System.
- Railroads, largely in private ownership, carry freight on 140,000 miles of track.
- Barge and ship lines utilize 12,000 miles of shallow-draft inland waterways and about 3,500 inland and coastal port terminal facilities.
- Air carriers provide cargo service to more than 5,000 public use airports, including more than 100 airports that handle all-cargo aircraft.

About two-fifths of freight within the United States, measured in ton-miles, moves by truck, and another two-fifths moves by rail (*Figure 1*). About

* This is an edited, reformatted and augmented version of a Congressional Research Service publication R42764, prepared for Members and Committees of Congress dated December 16, 2013.

11% moves by multiple modes. Measured in ton-miles, air transportation is a minor mode because it is expensive to ship goods this way. Goods moving by air tend to be of high value compared to their weight. About three-quarters of U.S. imports and exports, measured by weight, arrive or depart by ship. Most of the rest goes by truck (10%), rail (8%), or pipeline (5%). International air shipments account for less than 1% of U.S. foreign trade by weight, but 37% by value.[1]

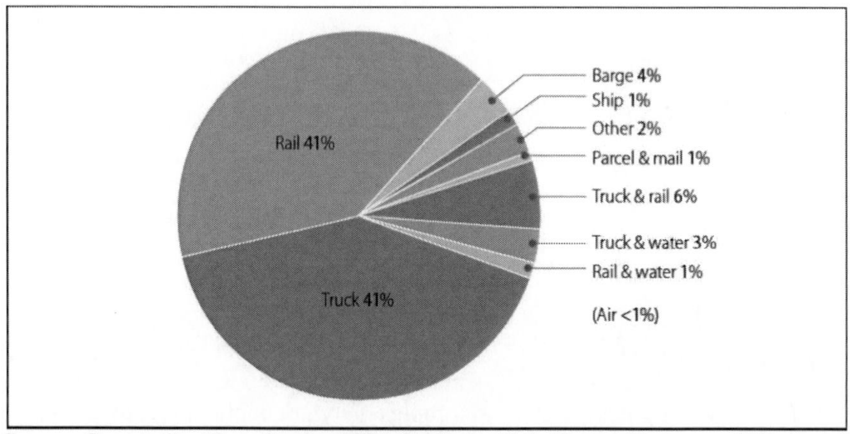

Source: Commodity Flow Survey 2007, Table 1a, U.S. Census Bureau and Bureau of Transportation Statistics. Survey covers U.S.-based shippers' outbound freight; it therefore excludes imports.

Note: One ton-mile equals one ton of freight shipped one mile.

Figure 1. Modal Shares of U.S. Freight. (Ton-miles).

THE FEDERAL ROLE IN PLANNING

The federal government does not have a direct role in freight infrastructure planning and project development. Decisions about investment in public freight-oriented infrastructure are made by state departments of transportation (state DOTs), metropolitan planning organizations (MPOs), and state or local entities such as port authorities. Private infrastructure decisions, such as construction of new railroad yards, are largely made by the companies themselves. Congress has long been concerned that state and local institutions have difficulty providing a comprehensive approach to improving freight movement: unlike commuter trips, which generally begin and end within a metropolitan area, freight trip lengths often exceed the jurisdiction of a single MPO or even a state, so action to relieve a freight bottleneck in one jurisdiction may merely shift the problem to another.

Allocating resources to freight at the federal level is difficult politically, for two reasons. First, it entails concentrating federal dollars in relatively few geographic areas. According to the American Trucking Associations, just 5% of the U.S. road system carries 75% of the nation's truck traffic.[2] One-third of all rail traffic passes through Chicago,[3] and while there are more than 40 U.S. container ports, 90% of the volume of containerized imports and exports is handled at just 10 ports.[4] Second, federal funding decisions in freight transportation have the potential to create winners and losers. For example, a federal expenditure to deepen one harbor but not another could shift the flow of freight and the location of business investments and jobs.

FEDERAL INITIATIVES AFFECTING FREIGHT FLOWS

Truck Chokepoints

The current federal freight transportation program is mainly a loose collection of highway-oriented programs embedded in a larger framework aimed at supporting both passenger and freight mobility. Highway-related programs are authorized by the Moving Ahead for Progress in the 21st Century Act, enacted in July 2012 (MAP-21; P.L. 112-141).[5]

Highway congestion frustrates trucking's ability to provide precise and reliable scheduling. Unreliability is costly because it requires manufacturers and retailers to carry buffer stock, reducing an efficient "just-in-time" (JIT) logistics strategy to a "just-in-case" strategy. The importance of predictability was highlighted in an article in *Public Roads*:[6] "From a freight perspective, the quintessential requirement for succeeding in a global, just-in-time economy is the ability to plan trips, deliveries, and transactions down to hours and minutes—rather than days and weeks. This makes reliability one of the single most important performance measures from a private sector perspective."

Most of the highway congestion points are at urban interchanges and at land border crossings. MAP-21 seeks to sharpen the focus on freight use of the highway system by identifying segments with the heaviest truck traffic, identifying truck chokepoints, regularly reporting on the condition and performance of these segments, and lowering the local cost share for freight-specific improvements.

Railroad Improvements

Railroads' decisions to invest in their infrastructure to improve transit times and schedule reliability are made on a commercial basis and do not always please shippers. Congress has sought to encourage investment in rail infrastructure through the Rail Rehabilitation and Improvement Financing (RRIF) program, which provides loans and credit assistance to sponsors of public and private rail projects. Eligible projects include acquiring, improving, or rehabilitating rail equipment, refinancing existing debt for these purposes, or developing new rail facilities. The 2005 transportation authorization act, the Safe, Accountable, Flexible, Efficient Transportation Equity Act: A Legacy for Users (P.L. 109-59), authorized $35 billion to provide direct loans and loan guarantees, with $7 billion of that amount reserved for railroads other than the seven Class I carriers.[7] Loans can be used to finance 100% of project costs with repayment up to 25 years. To date, almost all of the loan recipients have been shortline or regional railroads.[8]

In the past, Class I railroads proposed an infrastructure tax credit to allow them to reduce their tax burden for building new capacity. Shortline railroads seek a tax credit to rehabilitate existing facilities. Another legislative proposal that has been debated is the creation of a rail trust fund that would include a cargo waybill and passenger ticket tax as a means of generating revenue for railroad infrastructure investment. Freight railroads have opposed a rail trust fund arguing that taxing railroad use would not generate additional revenue for rail investment.

Positive Train Control

The Rail Safety Improvement Act of 2008 (RSIA08; P.L. 110-432) requires implementation of positive train control (PTC) on railroads that carry passengers or have high-volume freight traffic with toxic or poisonous-by-inhalation hazardous materials. PTC is a communications and signaling system that has been identified by the National Transportation Safety Board as a technology capable of preventing incidents caused by train operator or dispatcher error. PTC is expected to reduce the number of incidents due to excessive speed, conflicting train movements, and engineer failure to obey wayside signals. It would not prevent incidents due to trespassing on railroads' right-of-way or at highway-rail grade crossings, where the vast majority of rail-related fatalities occur.

Under RSIA08, PTC is required on about 60,000 miles of railroad track by December 31, 2015. Many railroad companies are uncertain of their ability to fully implement PTC by this deadline, and some contend that PTC implementation may divert resources from capacity expansion. The Federal Railroad Administration estimates full PTC implementation will cost approximately $14 billion. Although the larger freight railroads are well along in planning for PTC, some smaller railroads have not yet identified sources of funding for implementation. Congress is reevaluating the costs and benefits of PTC and the implementation deadline.[9]

Lock Maintenance

Locks on the inland waterways have become increasingly unreliable due to their age. Many were built in the 1930s and 1950s and require more frequent maintenance or major rehabilitation work by the Army Corps of Engineers. Federal funding for inland waterway infrastructure has not kept pace with increasing capital demands. Barge operators pay a 20-cent-per-gallon federal fuel tax that covers about one-tenth of the federal cost of providing inland navigation infrastructure. This user charge amounts to about 2% of the barge industry's freight revenues. A handful of waterway segments generate negligible traffic but consume about a third of the operating and maintenance budget.[10] Congress has been reluctant to require the waterway industry to provide more capital for the system's upkeep or to terminate federal support for uneconomic portions.[11]

Port Dredging

Enlargement of the Panama Canal, expected to be completed in early 2015, has spurred interest in deepening U.S. ports to accommodate larger ships. Yet only a handful of "load center" ports can realistically expect to see the larger ships. Under the present financing method and planning process, each port deepening project is initiated at the local level and evaluated in isolation from other port projects—no regional or national port rationalization strategy is part of the process. Ship operators pay none of the cost of dredging, so they do not consider this cost when calculating the costs and benefits of larger ships. Deepening projects are paid from the general fund. Maintenance dredging is financed by a federal tax primarily on imported waterborne cargo; however, only about a third of the revenue is used for cargo ports, with the remainder spent to maintain recreational and fishing harbors or on other government activities.[12]

Regulatory Points of Contention

Truck Size and Weight Limits

Current federal truck weight regulations restrict the maximum gross vehicle weight to 80,000 pounds.[13] An empty "18-wheeler" (five-axle tractor semi-trailer) typically weighs about 35,000 pounds, limiting the maximum cargo load to about 45,000 pounds. In addition to a maximum

gross vehicle weight, trucks also must comply with the "bridge formula," which sets weight limits on each axle depending on its distance to the next axle. Federal truck weight regulations apply only to the Interstate Highway System and to the roads that provide reasonable access to and from that system. Truck weight limits on all other highways and roads are regulated by the states.

Federal truck size regulations apply to the "National Network," a system of approximately 209,000 miles, which includes the Interstate Highway System plus principal arterial highways designated by the states and incorporated in federal regulations (23 C.F.R. §658). Federal regulations prescribe a width standard and minimum length standard, but no maximum length or height restrictions.[14] "Longer combination vehicles" (LCVs), which are trucks pulling two or more trailers with a gross vehicle weight exceeding 80,000 pounds, are allowed according to some states' broad interpretation of their "grandfathered" permit authority.

Large trucking firms and shippers support increasing truck size or weight limits, while small trucking firms, truck drivers, railroads, and highway safety groups are generally opposed. In MAP-21, Congress instructed the U.S. Department of Transportation (U.S. DOT) to perform a study of truck size and weight limits.[15]

"Captive" Rail Shippers

Some bulk rail shippers, particularly those that are served by one railroad, object to what they perceive as poor rail service and exorbitant rail rates. These "captive" shippers claim that the railroad serving them acts like a monopoly, charging excessive rates and providing less service than they require, because the railroad is aware that the cargo cannot be moved economically by truck. Some shipper interests want new federal laws or regulations requiring railroads to interchange cargo with one another at switching terminals so as to potentially increase competition. Currently, railroads interchange traffic at terminals only where they find it mutually beneficial to do so.

The Surface Transportation Board (STB), an independent agency organizationally housed within the U.S. DOT, has jurisdiction over railroad competition issues.[16] The STB has undertaken various investigations of captive shipper issues, but has not proposed broad changes in regulation.[17] Addressing the complaints of "captive" shippers may involve policy trade-offs, as railroads' freight revenues are a significant means of financing rail capacity, and a legislated or regulatory solution to the "captive shipper" problem could therefore affect the level of investment in the railroad system.[18]

The Jones Act

The Jones Act requires that cargo transported by water between two U.S. locations be carried in U.S.-built vessels, owned by and crewed by U.S. citizens.[19] The law, enacted in 1920 in response to a surplus of U.S.-built cargo ships from World War I, is intended to encourage U.S. shipbuilding and protect the jobs of U.S. merchant mariners. The United States is the only industrialized nation that has domestic build requirements for ships, and there is no similar requirement for most other modes of transportation.[20] The law's supporters contend it preserves shipbuilding capacity essential to national defense. Its critics say it has made the U.S. shipbuilding industry internationally uncompetitive: U.S.-built oceangoing cargo ships are said to be two to three times more expensive than foreign-built ships.[21]

Most shipping along the coasts of the mainland United States is conducted in oceangoing barges rather than in tankers or containerships that can carry far more cargo. Bulk shippers complain that high coastal water freight rates due to the Jones Act relieve competitive pressure on the railroads, raising transport costs on some routes. In 2013, oil industry representatives told a Senate committee the Jones Act was raising the cost and constraining the movement of crude oil from new domestic sources to U.S. coastal refineries.[22] Barges are widely used for coastal movement of crude oil and petroleum products, but they tend to be slower and less efficient than tankers. According to the

Maritime Administration, the capacity of tanker vessels eligible for Jones Act service fell by half between 2000 and 2013.[23]

The Jones Act may also facilitate collusion among carriers because the lack of available U.S.- built vessels inhibits entry by potential competitors. In 2011 and 2012, a U.S. Department of Justice investigation resulted in three container carriers paying $45 million in criminal fines and several executives receiving prison sentences.[24]

The President may waive the Jones Act when there is a sudden need for ships and no suitable U.S.-built vessels are available. Waivers were granted when hurricanes disrupted pipeline service in 2005 and, more recently, when the government released oil from the Strategic Petroleum Reserve.[25] In December 2012, Congress required the U.S. Maritime Administration and any federal agency requesting a Jones Act waiver to provide additional information, including an explanation of why the use of U.S.-built vessels is not feasible.[26]

End Notes

[1] For additional freight statistics, see U.S. Department of Transportation, Office of Freight Management and Operations, Freight Facts and Figures, issued annually, http://ops.fhwa.dot.gov/freight/.

[2] ATA, Transport Topics, December 8, 2008, p. 28.

[3] TRB, Rail Freight Solutions to Roadway Congestion—Final Report and Guidebook, NCHRP Report 586, 2007, p. 49.

[4] The Ports of Los Angeles and Long Beach and the Port of Seattle and Tacoma are counted as one port city. U.S. Department of Transportation, Maritime Administration, based on 2007 data.

[5] For further information on highway programs see CRS Report R42762, Surface Transportation Funding and Programs Under MAP-21: Moving Ahead for Progress in the 21st Century Act (P.L. 112-141), coordinated by Robert S. Kirk.

[6] U.S. Department of Transportation, Federal Highway Administration, "Reliability: Critical to Freight Transportation," Public Roads, vol. 68, no. 3, November/December 2004, p. 2.

[7] Class I railroads are the seven large, "mainline" railroads in North America. Class II railroads are regional railroads and Class III railroads are shortline railroads.

[8] For information on RRIF, including a list of loan recipients, see http://www.fra.dot.gov/rpd/freight/1770.shtml.

[9] See CRS Report R42637, Positive Train Control (PTC): Overview and Policy Issues, by John Frittelli.

[10] See Figure 5, p. 16 of CRS Report R41430, Inland Waterways: Recent Proposals and Issues for Congress, by Charles V. Stern.

[11] For further information, see CRS Report R43101, Inland Waterways: Financing and Management Options in Federal Studies, by John Frittelli.

[12] For further information, see CRS Report R43222, Harbor Maintenance Finance and Funding, by John Frittelli.

[13] Weight limits are promulgated at 23 U.S.C. §127; 23 C.F.R. 658.

[14] Size regulations are promulgated at 49 U.S.C. §§31111–31115; 23 C.F.R. 658.

[15] For further information on truck size and weight law, see http://ops. fhwa. dot.gov/freight/sw/index.htm.

[16] The STB was created in the Interstate Commerce Commission Termination Act of 1995 (P.L. 104-88).

[17] The STB has begun a proceeding examining competitive switching rules; see docket no. EP 711.

[18] See CRS Report RL34117, Railroad Access and Competition Issues, by John Frittelli.

[19] It is codified at 46 U.S.C. chapters 81, 121, and 551; 19 C.F.R. §§4.80 – 4.93; 46 C.F.R. §§67.19, 67.95-67.99.

[20] For instance, trucks, locomotives, and airplanes need not be domestically built. Certain domestic content requirements apply to federally funded purchases of mass transit vehicles and Amtrak rolling stock.

[21] "Can the Jones Act be Protected?," Journal of Commerce, December 5, 2011.

[22] Senate Committee on Energy and Natural Resources, Hearing to Explore the Effects of Ongoing Changes in Domestic Oil Production, Refining and Distribution on U.S. Gasoline and Fuel Prices, July 16, 2013.

[23] U.S. Maritime Administration, "2000-2013 U.S.-Flag Privately-Owned Fleet Summary," http://www.marad.dot.gov/ library_landing_page/data_and_statistics/Data_and_Statistics.htm#Fleet%20Statistics.

[24] U.S. Department of Justice press release, "Florida-Based Crowley Liner Services Inc. Pleads Guilty to Price Fixing on Freight Services Between U.S. and Puerto Rico," http://www. justice.gov/opa/pr/2012/August/12-at-962.html.

[25] The waiver process is codified at 46 U.S.C. §501.

[26] P.L. 112-213.

INDEX

D

E

F

G

M

N

O

P

Q

R

S

T

U

V

W

Y